Contents

Teachers' Notes

Introduction

The intention of this book is that it will be used as a stimulus, enabling teachers to experiment with and to feel the excitement that festivals can generate. The activities are not intended for any particular age group and indeed most of them can be adapted easily to meet individual and group needs.

Most of the necessary factual information concerning individual festivals can be found either within the activity sheets or in the teachers' notes. However, a number of books are listed at the end of this section if any further reading is required.

Every effort has been made to order the festivals according to their position in the school year. However, not all religions use the Gregorian calendar with which most of us are familiar. This means that many festival dates appear to move about from one year to the next. Where festivals have this 'moveable' characteristic they have been indicated with an **M** in the teachers' notes. To discover accurate dates teachers should consult the *Shap Festival Calendar* (see book list).

The spelling of many names connected with certain festivals tend to vary greatly from publication to publication. This can be explained by the number of translations that have taken place over the years. Whenever possible the spellings used in this book are in accordance with *Shap*.

Some teachers are often nervous about causing offence when they first introduce festivals that are new to them. The following general points should help to allay such worries.

- Don't assume that a child of a particular faith will know about all that faith's festivals.
- Be willing to ask parents and members of particular communities for assistance.
- Be prepared to admit that you are learning too. People are not likely to take offence if they know that you have an open mind.
- Do not allow any acting of the part of Sikh Gurus or portray animal and human forms in Islamic art.
- Festivals are fun, but remember that they are also religious and should be respected as such.

Autumn

Ethiopian New Year (Rastafarian)
11 September

Rastafarians name each year, in a four year cycle, after one of the apostles – Matthew, Mark, Luke and John.

Page 11: food that is suitable for a strict Rastafarian to eat is known as *Ital* food.

Navaratri/Durga Puja/Dessehra (Hindu) M

In India this festival is celebrated for nine days, but in Britain it is usually shortened. The festival commemorates Rama's conflict with Ravana, the Demon King, and the triumph of good over evil. It is celebrated with gurba dancing and the acting out of stories from the *Ramayana* (Holy Book).

Page 12: Alpana patterns are made as floor decorations with coloured powders.

Rosh Hashana (Jewish) M

The Jewish New Year marks the start of a period of self-examination. The ram's horn represents Abraham's sacrifice of a ram in place of his son. Traditionally, apples dipped in honey are eaten in anticipation of a sweet year ahead. Rosh Hashana is a time to repent and make amends.

Yom Kippur (Jewish) M

This festival marks the end of ten days of repentance. The day is spent fasting and praying in the synagogue and is the holiest day of the Jewish year. It is a time when people resolve to improve themselves and give to charity.

Page 17: 1 = Reading desk; 2 = Ten Commandments; 3 = Men's seats with women's above; 4 = Menorah; 5 = Bimah; 6 = Torah scrolls; 7 = Seat for wardens; 8 = Ner Tamid.

Harvest Festival (Christian) M

Festivals for harvest have been celebrated throughout time and all over the world. In Medieval Britain people used to celebrate Lammas Day. They would bless bread which had been made from the first corn harvest.

Page 22: while it is interesting for children to know from where foods originate, they should realise that our gain is often at a cost to someone else.

Page 23: the traditional view of harvest can be quite remote to many inner city children. Try to make the topic relevant to all children by, for example, examining the many processes and people involved in getting the food from the field to the table.

Page 24: this festival is celebrated in West Africa by both Christians and Muslims. It is characterised by dancing, drumming, wearing masks and feasting.

Page 25: most of these breads can be obtained easily from large supermarkets and delicatessens. More difficult ones such as har-do can be bought from specialist Caribbean shops, while the children can make others such as chapatti.

Cottage loaf = English; harvest loaf = English; matzah = Israeli; baguette = French; naan = Pakistani; har-do = Caribbean; chapatti = Indian; challah = ; bread sticks = Italian; pitta = Greek; garlic bread = French; sliced loaf= English.

Thanksgiving (Christian) November M

Thanksgiving is usually associated with turkey and pumpkin pie. However, not all Americans feel that it is a cause for celebration. We should ask children to examine this festival from the point of view of the native Americans.

Page 26: perhaps the children could consider how Chief Massasoit would feel if he could see what is happening in America to native Americans today.

Sukkot (Jewish) M
This nine day festival is known as the Feast of Tabernacles. By building temporary shelters called *sukkahs*, Jewish people are reminded of the protection they received when they were travelling in the wilderness for 40 years. They also wave myrtle branches to symbolise palm, willow and etrog (fruit of the citron tree) to show that God is everywhere.
Page 27: these models can be made in a variety of sizes by individuals or groups of children.
Simkhat Torah (Jewish) M
This celebration takes place at the end of Sukkot and is a very joyous occasion. The last section of Deuteronomy is read from the Torah and another scroll started to show the continuity of the Torah. All the scrolls are paraded around the synagogue seven times, with the children singing and dancing behind them.
Page 28: the size of the Torah and the materials it is made from can vary. Remember that the Torah is only touched with a pointer and that it would be read from right to left.
Eid Miald-un-Nabi (Islam) M
This is the celebration of Muhammad's birthday. It is usually a solemn occasion when stories of the Prophet are told and lectures given.
Page 29: remember that living creatures are not portrayed in Islamic art.
Kathina (Buddhist) M
This is a time when new robes are presented to monks by lay people. The festival takes place at the end of the rainy season, three months after Asalha Puja (see page 139).
Page 30: there are several Buddhist monasteries in Britain and an increasing number of children's books on Buddhism.
Divali (Hindu) M
The name Divali means 'a row of lights'. It commemorates the story of Rama and Sita, but it is also a celebration of the New Year and a time when business people examine their accounts and worship Lakshmi, the Goddess of wealth. Divali is celebrated with decorations, gifts and cards. In some British cities such as Leicester, streets are also decorated.
Pages 38 to 43: use these figures to make stick puppets, silhouettes or as a basis for illustrations.
Divali (Sikh) M
Sikhs celebrate this festival by visiting the *gurdwara* (Sikh temple) and decorating their homes with lights. It was at this time that the sixth Guru, Hargobind Singh, was released from prison.
All Saints' Day (Christian) 1 November
This day is intended to be a time when all Christian saints are remembered.
Birthday of Guru Nanak (Sikh) November M
Guru Nanak is the founder of the Sikh religion. His birthday is an important festival and is celebrated at the gurdwara by reading the *Guru Granth Sahib* from beginning to end. This takes three days and is called *Akhand Path*. At this celebration food is also shared in the *langhar* (free kitchen). In some areas there might also be street processions.
Crowning of Haile Selassie (Rastafarian) 2 November
This is one of the holiest days of the Rastafarian year and it celebrates Haile Selassie's accession to the Ethiopian throne. It is celebrated by drumming, chanting and feasts.
Page 50: (see opposite for the word search solution).
St Andrew's Day (Christian) 30 November
St Andrew is the patron saint of Scotland. He was one of the disciples of Jesus and St Peter's brother. His relics were taken to Scotland in the thirteenth century. It is thought that he was crucified on an 'x' shaped cross.
Page 51: this assembly sheet can be used to form the basis of a poster or invitation to an assembly.

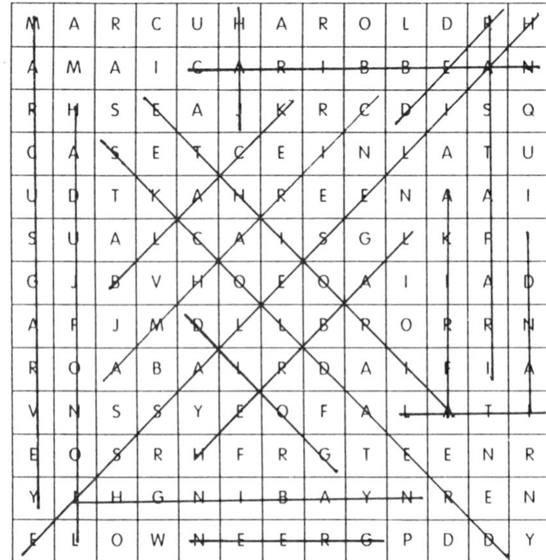

Loy Krathong (Theravada Buddhist) M
This festival is also known as the 'Floating Candle Festival'. The Buddha compared Buddhist teaching to a raft which carries you across the river of ignorance – meaning that following the Buddhist teaching will allow you to find truth. It is a time for giving thanks to and asking forgiveness of the water spirits.
Sangha Day (Buddhist) M
The Buddha taught about harmony. This is linked with the meditation practice called *metta* (loving kindness) which concentrates thoughts on loving kindness to others. Celebrations might include a firework display.
Advent (Christian) M
The Christian year begins on Advent Sunday. Advent lasts for four weeks and is a time of spiritual preparation for Christmas. This 'countdown to Christmas' is often marked with Advent calendars, wreaths and candles.

Hanukah (Jewish) M
This festival lasts for eight days and a candle is lit each evening. It reminds Jews of the time when there was only enough oil left to keep the temple light burning for one day, but it miraculously stayed alight for eight days. (A light is still kept burning continuously in synagogues today.)
Page 55: the writing says Happy Hanukah in Hebrew.
Page 59: the Hebrew words on the dreidel mean 'a great miracle happened there'. To play the game each child should be given an equal number of counters. Each player should then place one counter in the centre to form a 'pot'. The first player spins the dreidel and obeys the instruction. The game continues in this manner. The winner is the child who ends up with all the counters.
Christmas (Christian) 25 December
Christmas is the celebration of the birth of Christ. The exact date of Christ's birth is not known and so the Orthodox Church celebrates Christmas on 6 January. At Christmas Christians exchange gifts and cards, go to church, sing carols and take part in general festivities. Children often depict Christ as one of their own heritage group, but it is important to remind them that He would have resembled the people of the area in which He lived and would not have been white or pink as often illustrated by many children.
Page 62: orange = the world; candle = the light of the world; red ribbon = the blood of Christ; four cocktail sticks = the four seasons; nuts and dried fruit = the fruits of the earth.
New Year 1 January
This is a time when people consider making a fresh start and make various resolutions.
Page 68: this is traditionally sung on New Year's Eve. Friends link arms and sing together.
Birthday of Guru Gobind Singh (Sikh) M
Guru Gobind Singh was the tenth and last Guru. He abolished the caste system and encouraged equality of opportunity. He gave final form to the Sikh faith and created Khalsa by baptising the five Pyares (beloved ones) on Baisakhi in 1699.
Page 70: this quote can be enlarged and used for display purposes or to initiate discussion on equal opportunities.
Epiphany (Christian) 6 January
Epiphany takes place 12 days after Christmas and celebrates the time when the Magi gave gifts to Christ.

Spring

Basant (Sikh) M
This festival takes place at the beginning of spring. In the Punjab kite flying competitions take place and people wear yellow.
Saraswati Puja (Hindu) M
Saraswati Puja is dedicated to Saraswati, the Goddess of learning and the arts.
Yuan Tan (Chinese) M
This festival celebrates the New Year. Blossom trees and dragons are symbols of good luck and 'lucky bags' containing money are given as gifts to children at this time. The colours gold and red predominate. New Year might also be celebrated with fireworks or dances such as the famous lion dance. It is also a time when business accounts are settled.
Pages 74 to 79: the years are named after animals and it is thought that people take on certain characteristics according to the year in which they are born. It may be necessary to check before using horoscopes as some parents do not agree with using them in any form.
Shrove Tuesday (Christian) M
This is traditionally a time when rich foods were used up prior to fasting in Lent. People were thought to be 'shrove' after they had confessed. Pancake races take place at this time.
Carnival (Christian) M
Mardi gras traditionally took place on Shrove Tuesday. It was taken to the Caribbean and South America by Europeans, but not all islands celebrate carnival. Jamaica only celebrated its first carnival in the 1990s. Associated with carnival is the development of steel-drum music.
Lent (Christian) M
Ash Wednesday marks the beginning of Lent. It gets its name from the burning of the previous year's palms (see Palm Sunday). The ashes are then sprinkled with holy water and used to mark a cross on the heads of the congregation. This cross used to be seen as a sign of penance. Lent is a reminder of the 40 days Christ spent in the wilderness. It is a period of spiritual preparation for Easter. Many Christians deny themselves some luxuries or foods during this time.
St David's Day (Christian) 1 March
St David is the patron saint of Wales. The saint's day has been celebrated since the fourteenth century. He lived in South-West Wales and was Archbishop. Welsh people wear leeks and daffodils on this day.
Page 86: this assembly sheet can be used to form the basis of a poster or invitation to a St David's Day assembly.
Holi (Hindu) M
The story of Holi illustrates God's protection of believers. Celebrations are colourful and joyful. Festivities include dances, throwing coloured powder and water and processions, and are a reminder of Krishna's games. The story of Holi can be told using puppets, shadow puppets, dance and drama.
Holla Mahalla (Sikh) M
This festival has its roots in the Hindu festival of Holi. Guru Gobind Singh introduced this festival as a Sikh alternative to Holi and used it as training for the army. It included music, poetry, sport and military exercises.

Purim (Jewish) M
Purim celebrates the time when Queen Esther saved the Jews of Persia from being killed by Haman's plotting. The Book of Esther is read in the synagogue and whenever Haman's name is mentioned the congregation stamp their feet and boo and hiss to drown the sound of Haman's name.
Hina Matsuri (Japanese) M
This festival is also known as 'Girls' Day' or 'Dolls' Day'. It originated at a time when it was believed that dolls drove away evil spirits. Nowadays, Japanese girls display dolls draped with red cloth.
Page 96: use this sheet to make posters or invitations.
Sangkran (Buddhist) 13 to 16 April
Sangkran is the Thai New Year and Water Festival. It is celebrated with shadow puppets and the setting free of caged birds and fish. It is also traditional to throw scented water over an image of the Buddha and to pour it over the hands of the monks.
Mothering Sunday (Christian) M
Traditionally, Mothering Sunday was a time when people visited their mothers and their 'mother church'. Children gave their mothers posies of violets. Care must be taken that assumptions are not made about who plays the 'mothering role' within the family.
St Patrick's Day (Christian) 17 March
St Patrick is the patron saint of Ireland. He was a fourth-century priest and missionary. He is supposed to have rid Ireland of snakes. He tricked the last one into a box and threw the box into the sea. On this day Irish people might wear the symbol of the shamrock.
Page 100: this assembly sheet can be used to form the basis of a poster or invitaion to an assembly.
Ramadan (Islam) M
This is a special month during which the Qu'ran was revealed. Muslims fast from dawn to dusk as a way of thanks. It is a period of self-discipline and gives ordinary people an experience of poverty.
Page 101: this activity should help children to understand the lunar calendar.
Rama Navami (Hindu) M
Rama Navami is a day celebrated by fasting and visiting decorated temples. It commemorates the birth of Rama. Cradles are made and the image of the infant Rama uncovered at mid-day.
Page 102: this might be an appropriate time to visit a Hindu *mandir* (temple). Letters similar to this might be used for other visits.
Hanamatsuri (Zen Buddhist) 8 April
Zen Buddhists use this flower festival to celebrate the birthday of the Buddha. Flowers are a reminder that the Buddha is said to have been born in a garden called Lumbini. He was born, enlightened and died under a tree.
Page 103: the lotus flower is placed around the image of the Buddha. It reminds Buddhists of the teachings of Buddha. This is because at first the lotus bud has its roots in mud like a baby beginning life. The flower then begins to rise through the water like a child at school. Once it is above water the petals on the flower start to open. The flower is then like someone who has learned how to live successfully with all creatures.
Palm Sunday (Christian) M
This is the first day of 'Holy Week' and it commemorates Christ's triumphal journey to Jerusalem where He was welcomed by crowds waving palms. It is celebrated with church processions and the distribution of palm crosses.
Pesach (Jewish) M
The Passover story is told in the Book of Exodus. It celebrates the Israelites' freedom from slavery. Jewish people remember this story at Pesach (Passover). They clean their homes and gather together to share the *Seder* – a very special gathering and meal where the *Haggadah* is read. This is a small book which tells the story of the escape from slavery. The reading is introduced by the youngest child asking four questions, the first one being, 'Why is this night different from all other nights?'

Passover celebrations go on for eight days, during which time *matzah* is eaten. This is a reminder of the unleavened bread which was eaten on the journey to freedom when there wasn't enough time to let it rise.

There are more traditions associated with Pesach such as the search for the *afikoman* (a specially wrapped piece of matzah).
Page 106: 1 = The Israelites' freedom from slavery; 2 = Blood, frogs, lice, wild beasts, blight, boils, hail, locusts, darkness, death of the firstborn; 3 = Moses; 4 = A special plate that holds the symbolic foods of the Passover meal; 5 = Matzahs, shankbone of lamb, egg, maror (bitter herbs), charoset, wine, salt water, green vegetables such as parsley; 6 = The youngest child present; 7 = Four; 8 = A book which contained the story of the Exodus plus comments and teachings by several rabbis. It means 'the telling'; 9 = To remove any traces of unleavened bread; 10 = Matzah.
Page 108: Bitter herbs = A reminder of the hard times faced by the Israelites in Egypt; Charoset = A reminder of the cement used to build palaces and cities in Egypt; Salt water = A reminder of the taste of the Israelites tears; Cup of wine = A symbol of joy and freedom; Roasted egg = A symbol of new life and a reminder of the festival offerings in the last temple; Matzah = To remember the speed at which the Israelites left Egypt - they didn't even have enough time to let their bread rise; Shank bone of lamb = Represents the Paschal lamb which would have been sacrificed in gratitude; Cushions on chairs = A symbol of relaxation after slavery; Green herbs =

A sign of spring and a reminder of God's provision of food.

Baisakhi (Sikh) 13 or 14 April

This festival takes place at harvest time and New Year in the Punjab. It is celebrated with *bhangra* dancing, singing and visiting the gurdwara.

Pages 111 and 112: children can match the descriptions with the illustrations. The turban is not one of the five Ks – it is the uncut hair that is important. Until old enough to wear a turban a boy is likely to wear a patka or handkerchief on his head. A baptised Sikh would wear all five symbols.

When they first came to Britain in the 1950s many Sikhs cut their hair. Children can discuss why they did this and how they must have felt about this attempt at being accepted.

Easter (Christian) M

This is the most important festival of the Christian year. The word 'Easter' comes from the Anglo-Saxon 'Eostre' and it is possible that the festival might have displaced a pagan one. The tradition of giving eggs as a sign of new life is also an ancient one. The 'Easter story' is well documented. In these activities it is hoped that the children will be reminded of the religious significance of the festival as well as Easter eggs.

Page 113: this sheet should be copied and cut into nine rectangles for a small group of children. They should then put the cards in the correct order and decide how they would like to convey the story to their class.

Page 114: try to get the children to see the same story from different points of view.

Summer

Ridvan (Baha'i) 21 April to 2 May

Ridvan is a 12 day festival which celebrates the time, in 1863, when Baha'u'llah announced himself to be a Messenger of God. He had been exiled from Iran to Baghdad in 1853 and his fame had spread far and wide. The Muslim authorities were concerned about this popularity and decided to exile him again. Before he left, Baha'u'llah visited a garden and spent 12 days there. The people of Baghdad were sad to see him go and so he was visited by many followers. It was so windy that his followers had to sit on the ropes of his tent, to stop it from blowing away. The river Tigris rose so that his family were unable to join him until the ninth day. The whole family then left for Constantinople on the twelfth day. It was during this time that Baha'u'llah announced that he was the 'Promised one'.

Baha'is elect their Local Spritual Assemblies on the first day of Ridvan each year. These assemblies decide on what should be done for the community. But for children, far more important is the party which many Baha'i communities hold.

Page 117: it would be useful to discuss the use of out-of-date and stereotypical images when introducing this activity.

St George's Day (Christian) 23 April

St George is the patron saint of England. There are many legends about him but very few facts are known. George was martyred in Palestine and may have been a soldier in the Roman army. The story of God giving him the strength to kill the dragon is well known. The rose might be worn as a symbol on this day and members of scouting groups hold parades.

Page 118: this assembly sheet can be used to form the basis of a poster or invitation to an assemly.

May Day 1 May

May Day celebrations can be traced back to Roman times with the Festival of Maia, the mother of Mercury. The custom of dancing round a maypole probably began in Medieval times. Celebrations were forbidden under Cromwell but revived by Charles II. In the nineteenth century, May Day became known as Labour Day. Many May Day traditions have died out, but locals may remember some of them.

Wesak/Vaisakha Puja (Therevada Buddhist) M

This is probably the most important festival for Therevada Buddhists. It commemorates the Buddha's birth, enlightenment and death. It is marked by decorating homes and visiting temples or monasteries. In some countries there are street processions and entertainments. It is a colourful and happy festival. It is traditional to circumambulate a temple or monastery three times, remembering each of the three jewels of Buddhism – the Buddha, the Dhama and the Sangha.

Page 120: copy this sheet on to flame-coloured paper before using it. All the flames can be used to make a wall display.

Boys' Day (Japanese) 5 May

This is a festival which began after the Second World War. In Japan, gardens are decorated with streamers in the shape of carp (a fish with great energy and determination) and pin-wheels.

Lailat-ul-Qadr (Muslim) M

This is the 27th night of Ramadan during which the Qu'ran was revealed to Muhammad. This night is spent remembering Allah.

Eid-ul-Fitr (Muslim) M

This festival is celebrated at the end of Ramadan when the new moon is sighted. There is great celebration after fasting. Muslims attend the mosque and visit families and exchange gifts and cards.

Shavuot (Jewish) M

This is a celebration of the giving of the Ten Commandments. It is associated with harvest and the synagogue is decorated with flowers and fruit.

Whitsun/Pentecost (Christian) M

At Whitsun Christians celebrate the time when the Holy Spirit was given to the followers of Christ. The receivers were said to have talked 'in tongues'. It was at the time of the Jewish festival of Pentecost but became known as the birthday of the Christian Church. It probably became known as 'Whit' Sunday because it was a popular day for baptism when people wore white. Celebrations vary according to local custom and include such things as well dressing and Whit walks.

Page 130: size and degree of difficulty can be changed to suit the children and available material.

Dragon Boat Festival (Chinese) M

Dragon boat races take place annually in Hong Kong between long narrow boats which are decorated to resemble dragons. The colours red and gold predominate.

Trinity Sunday (Christian) M

This is day when Christians consider the time when God was revealed as Father, Son and Holy Ghost. Some people find this concept hard to understand, but the example of water can be used to help clarify this concept as we accept that water can be solid, liquid or gas.

Jagannath/Ratha Yatra (Hindu) M

This festival is celebrated in many areas of India, but chiefly in Puri where people carry images of Krishna on huge chariots. Krishna is celebrated as Jagannatha, 'Lord of the Universe' and it is from this that we get the word 'juggernaut'.

Page 134: anorak = Inuit; shampoo = Hindi; bungalow = Hindi; chocolate = Nauhati (Aztec); ukelele = Hawaiian; slogan = Gaelic; yoghurt = Turkish; cargo = Spanish; typhoon = Chinese; poodle = German; robot = Czech; hiccup = Dutch; garage = French; piano = Italian; carnival = Italian; blonde = French.

Eid-ul-Adha (Muslim) M

Eid-ul-Adha is a festival of sacrifice and is celebrated at the end of *Hajj* (pilgrimage to Mekka). Muslims try to make this pilgrimage to Mekka at least once during their lives. It is a time when all participants are regarded as equal. This festival is a solemn time which is associated with the story of Ibrahim (Abraham). It is told both in the Qu'ran and in the Bible. Ibrahim had a vision which told him that he should sacrifice his son and because he was willing to carry out this instruction, God saved the life of his son. Muslims now sacrifice animals at this time and give one third of the meat to the poor.

Page 137: 1 = as a symbol of giving everything up; 2 = to show that they are all equal; 3 = seven times; 4 = a stone believed to have been part of the Ka'aba built by Abraham; 5 = the well of Zam Zam; 6 = as they walk around the Ka'aba.

Dhamma Day/Asalha Puja (Therevada Buddhist) M

Dhamma Day celebrates the first sermon of Gautama (the Buddha) when the Wheel of Truth or Teaching was first taught in the Deer Park at Sarnath to the five ascetics with whom he had fasted. This festival falls just before the beginning of Vassa.

Page 139: 1 = Judaism; 2 = Judaism or Rastafariansim; 3 = Christianity; 4 = Islam; 5 = Sikhism; 6 = Hinduism.

Birthday of Haile Selassie (Rastafarian) 23 July

Haile Selassie's birthday is celebrated by lectures (referred to as reasonings), films, exhibitions, African dance, and drumming, reggae music and parties. The whole family takes part in the singing and dancing plus eating Ital food.

Raksha Bandhan (Hindu) M

This is a very old custom in which girls put *rakhi* (red and gold amulets) around the wrists of their brothers as a protection from evil. They might also tie them around the wrists of close family. In return, the boys give their sisters gifts.

Ganesh-Chaturthi (Hindu) M

This celebrates the birthday of Ganesh. Ganesh is associated with the removal of obstacles. ('The Wise Men and the Elephant' is from *Poems for You*, Book IV published by V. R. Sibley (last two verses by Mrs J. M. Biart) by permission of *RE Today*.)

Page 143: the children can record the six items that the blind men thought they felt. They can then discuss ways in which we can view issues and situations in different ways.

Janamastami (Hindu) M

This is the celebration of Krishna's birthday. Many Hindus fast before midnight when the celebrations begin. Often, homes are decorated and an image of Krishna is placed in a cradle.

Book list

Series

'Celebrations' series, A & C Black.
'Explore a Theme' series, CEM.
'Festival' series, Macmillan.
'Festivals' series, Wayland.
'The Living Festivals' series, REMP, Chansitor Publications.
'Looking at Festivals' series, Lutterworth Press.
'Religion through Festivals' series, Longman.
'Seasonal Activities' series, Wayland.

Books, magazines and poster packs

Chinese New Year, Minority Group Support Service, Coventry LEM.
Christmas around the World, Minority Group Support Service, Coventry LEM.
Dates and Meanings of Religious and Other Festivals, John Walshe, Foulsham.
Divali, Minority Group Support Service, Coventry LEM.
Festivals and Special Days Poster Pack, Philip Green.
The Jewish Kids Catalog, The Jewish Publications Society of America.
Projects for Winter; *Projects for Spring*; *Projects for Summer*;
Projects for Autumn; Celia McInnes, Wayland.
RE Today (magazine), CEM.
Shap Calendar of Religious Festivals, Shap Working Party, Hobsons.

Name ____________________

A Rastafarian feast

Some Rastafarians have very strict dietary rules, for example not eating meat, preservatives, additives, added salt, or alcohol and only eating organically grown food.

✤ Make a list of all the food that you have eaten in the last 24 hours.

✤ Highlight the ones that could be eaten by a strict Rastafarian.

✤ Plan a menu for a New Year's party for a strict Rastafarian.

Name ____________________

Alpana patterns

Alpana patterns are made as floor decorations during this festival. These are some examples.

✤ Make up some of your own patterns.

Model of Ravana

Ravana is depicted as an evil demon with many heads who was conquered by Prince Rama.

✤ Work in small groups to design and make a model of how you think he might have looked. Use this template to help you.

✤ Will each face have the same expression?

Name ____________

Greetings card

Rosh Hashana reminds Jews that Abraham was willing to sacrifice his son if God wished. God saved his life and a ram was sacrificed instead. The ram's horn is a symbol of the festival.

✤ Design a greetings card for the festival of Rosh Hashana.

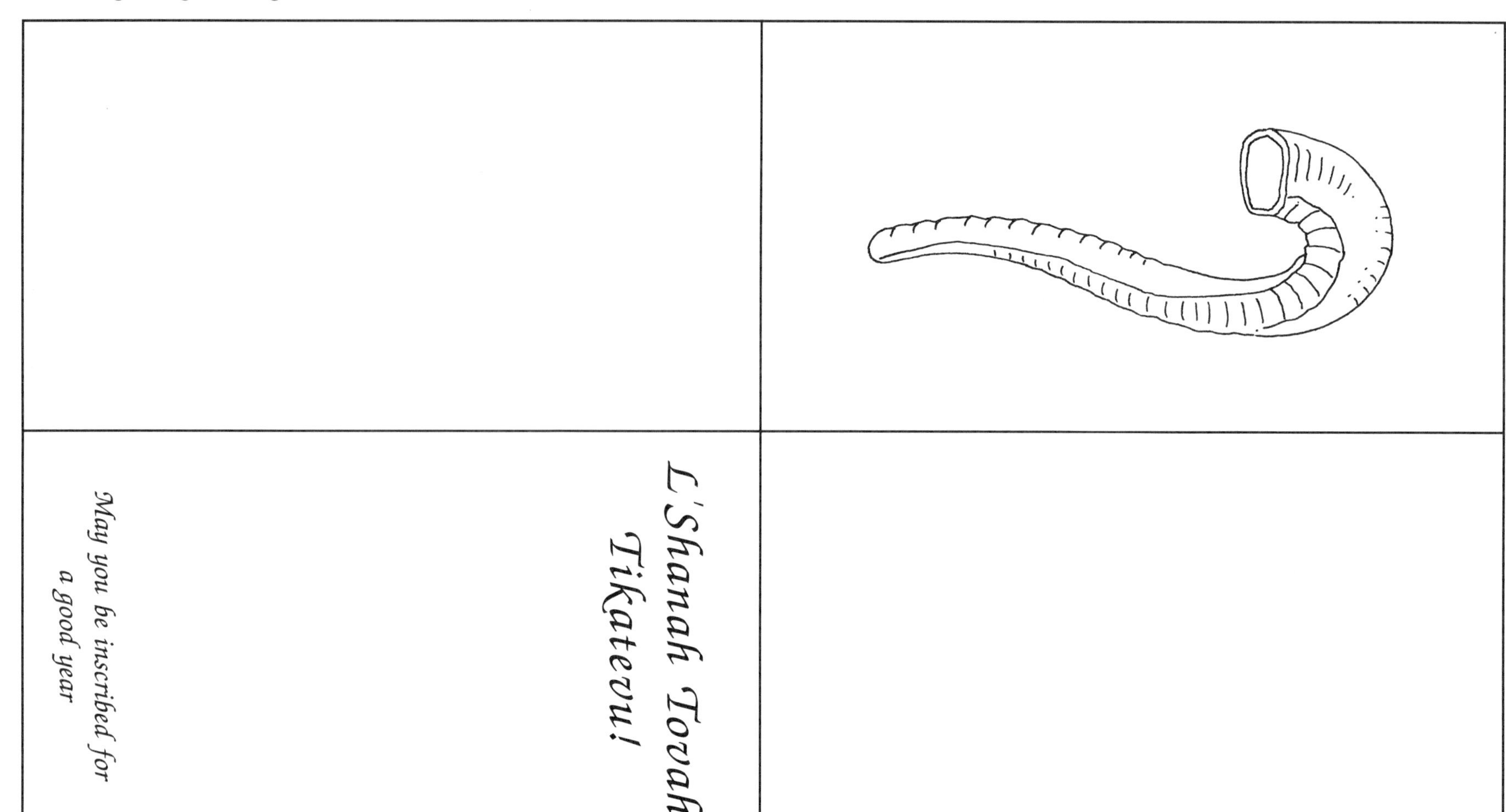

I can do better

At this time of year Jewish people think about things they have done during the past year and about ways to improve.

✤ Think about things that you can try to do better.

I CAN...	
What I do now	**How I will try to improve**

Name ____________

Honey cake

Honey is eaten at this time in the hope that the year ahead will be sweet.
✤ Follow this recipe to make your own honey cake.
Remember to wash your hands first and let an adult take the hot pan out of the oven.

What you need
- 2½ cups flour
- ¾ cup honey
- 1 cup sugar
- ½ cup oil
- ½ cup cool strong coffee
- 2 eggs
- 1 tsp of baking powder
- 1 tsp of baking soda
- 1 tsp of cinnamon
- a few sliced almonds
- loaf pan 23cm x 13cm
- waxed paper
- mixing bowls
- measuring and mixing spoons
- skewer to test the cake is cooked

What to do
- Prepare the tin and line it with paper. Set the oven at 160°C or gas mark 3.
- Beat the eggs until they are frothy. Slowly add the honey, sugar and oil, mixing all the time.
- In a separate bowl, mix the dry ingredients. They need to be well mixed together.
- Add half the coffee and half the dry mixture to the eggs. Mix well, then add the rest. Mix until smooth.
- Pour the mixture into the loaf pan and sprinkle the almonds on top.
- Cook for approximately 1 hour. To test whether the cake is ready poke a skewer into the cake and see if it comes out clean.
- Wash up.

Name ____________________

The Orthodox synagogue

Below is a plan of a synagogue.
✤ Match each object with its name and write the numbers beside them.
✤ Find out what each object is used for.

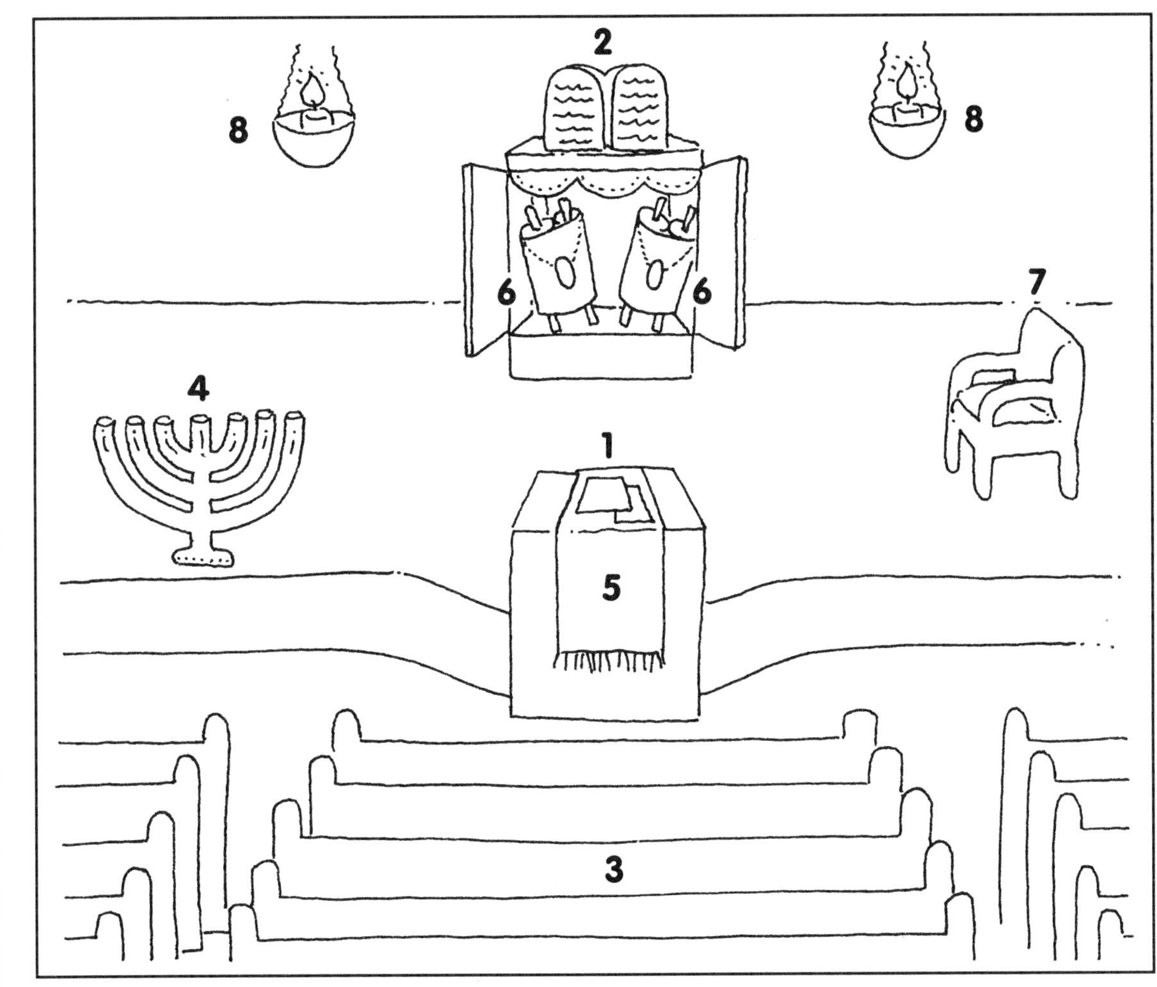

_______ Ner Tamid (eternal light)

_______ Ten Commandments

_______ Torah scrolls in the Ark

_______ Menorah

_______ Seat for wardens

_______ Reading desk

_______ Bimah

_______ Men's seats with seats for women in the gallery above.

Name ____________________

The growth of a bean

If you grow a bean in a clear container you will be able to observe its growth.

✤ Plot the growth of the stem and root on the graph below.

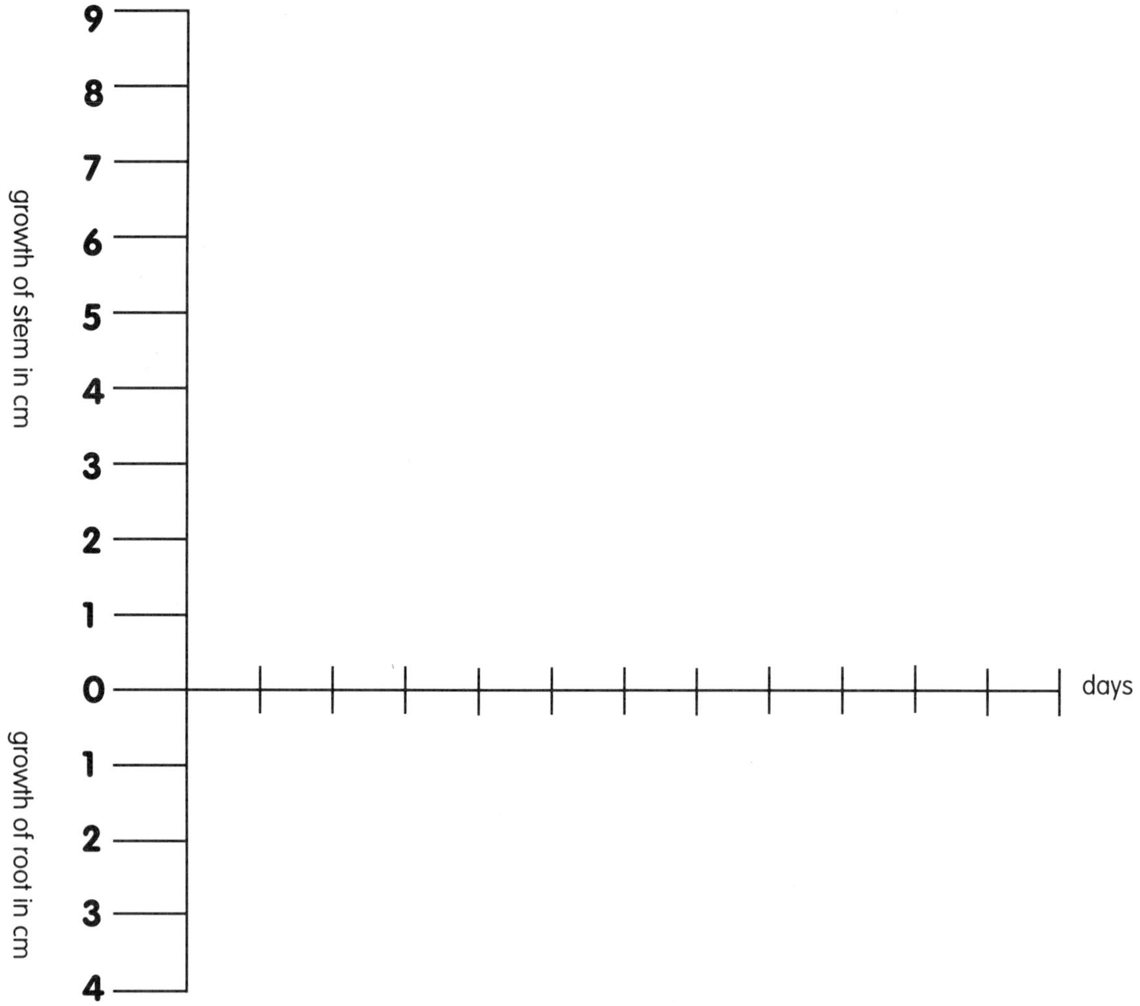

growth of stem in cm: 9, 8, 7, 6, 5, 4, 3, 2, 1, 0

days

growth of root in cm: 1, 2, 3, 4

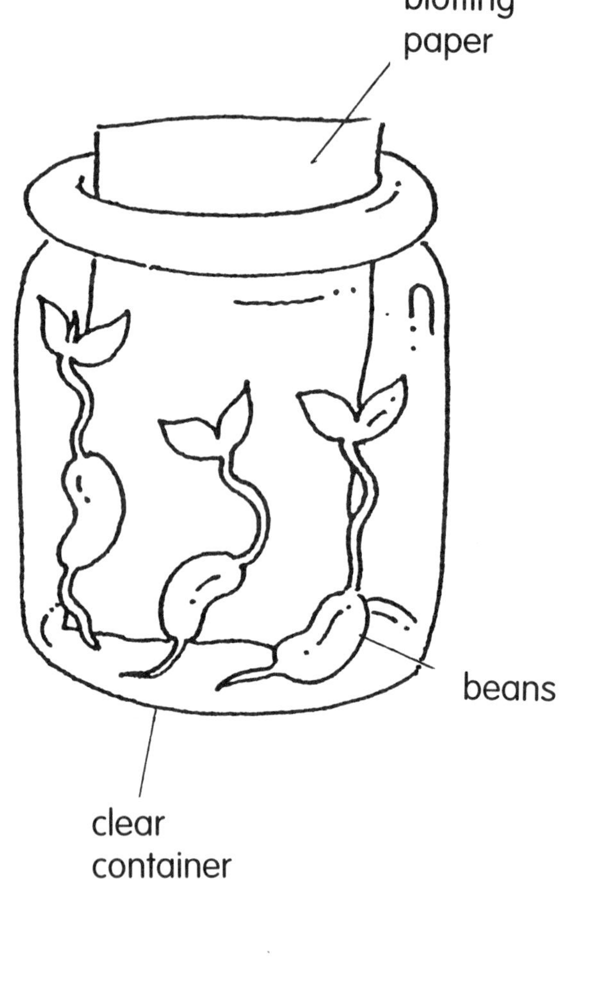

Horn of plenty or cornucopia

A cornucopia is a traditional harvest decoration.

✤ Follow the instructions to make your own horn of plenty as shown in the illustration below.

- Decorate the sheet
- Fold the sheet into a horn shape by sticking face A on to face B.
- Stick the flat base (AB) on to thick card.
- Fill your horn with ears of corn, grasses, Plasticine fruits and so on.

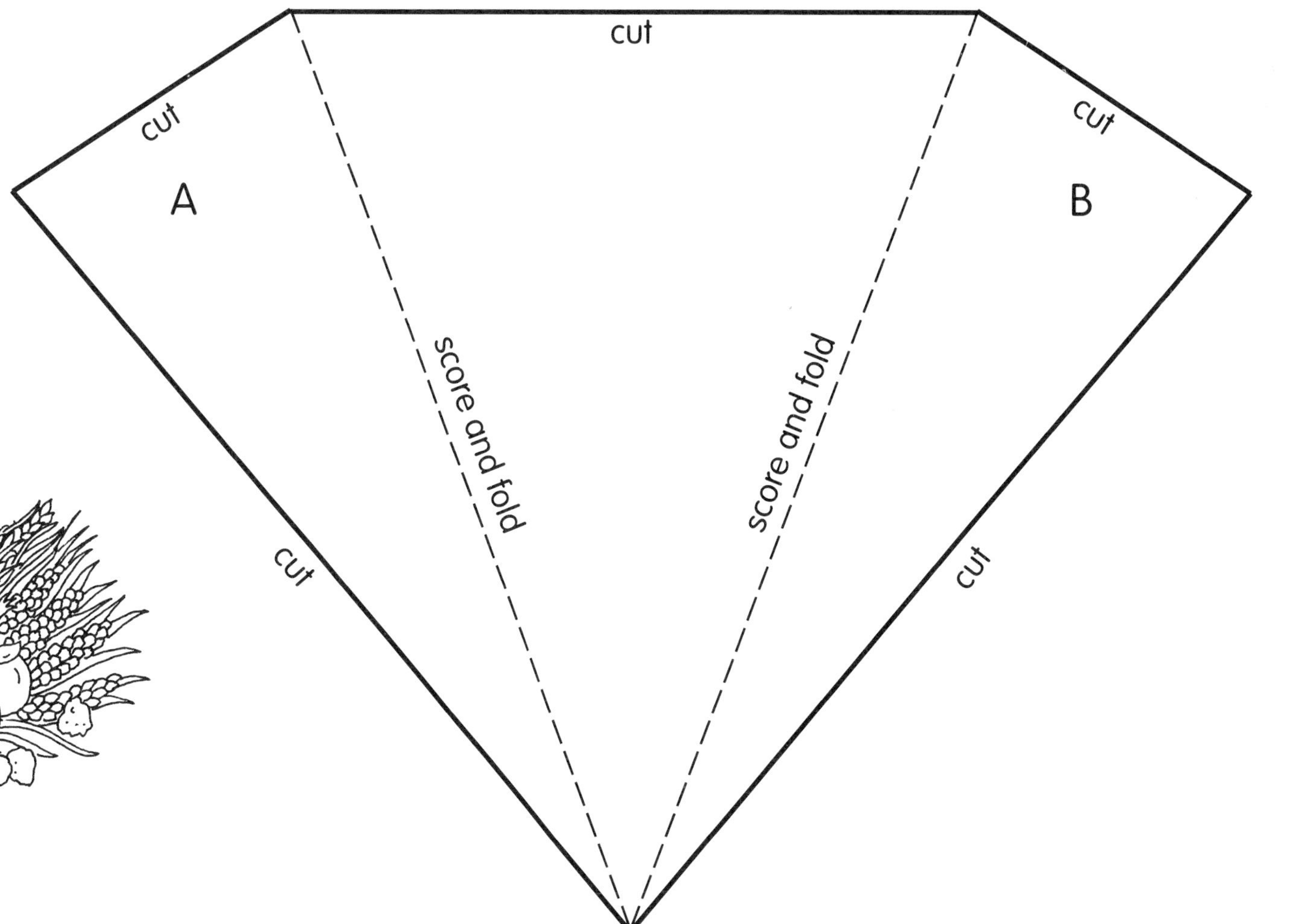

Name ______________________

Other times, other places

- Work in groups to find out about different harvest customs, both in the past and from around the world.
- Write down what you find out below and then share this with the rest of the class.

Country of origin

✤ Visit a supermarket and make a list of the country of origin for different items.
✤ Record them on this sheet.

Item	Country of origin	Item	Country of origin

✤ Mark the countries of origin on a map of the world.

Name ____________________

Sharing the banana

If you spend £1 on Jamaican bananas, 88½p stays in Britain for the dockers, carriers, shippers and retailers. Only 11½p goes to Jamaica for the growers.

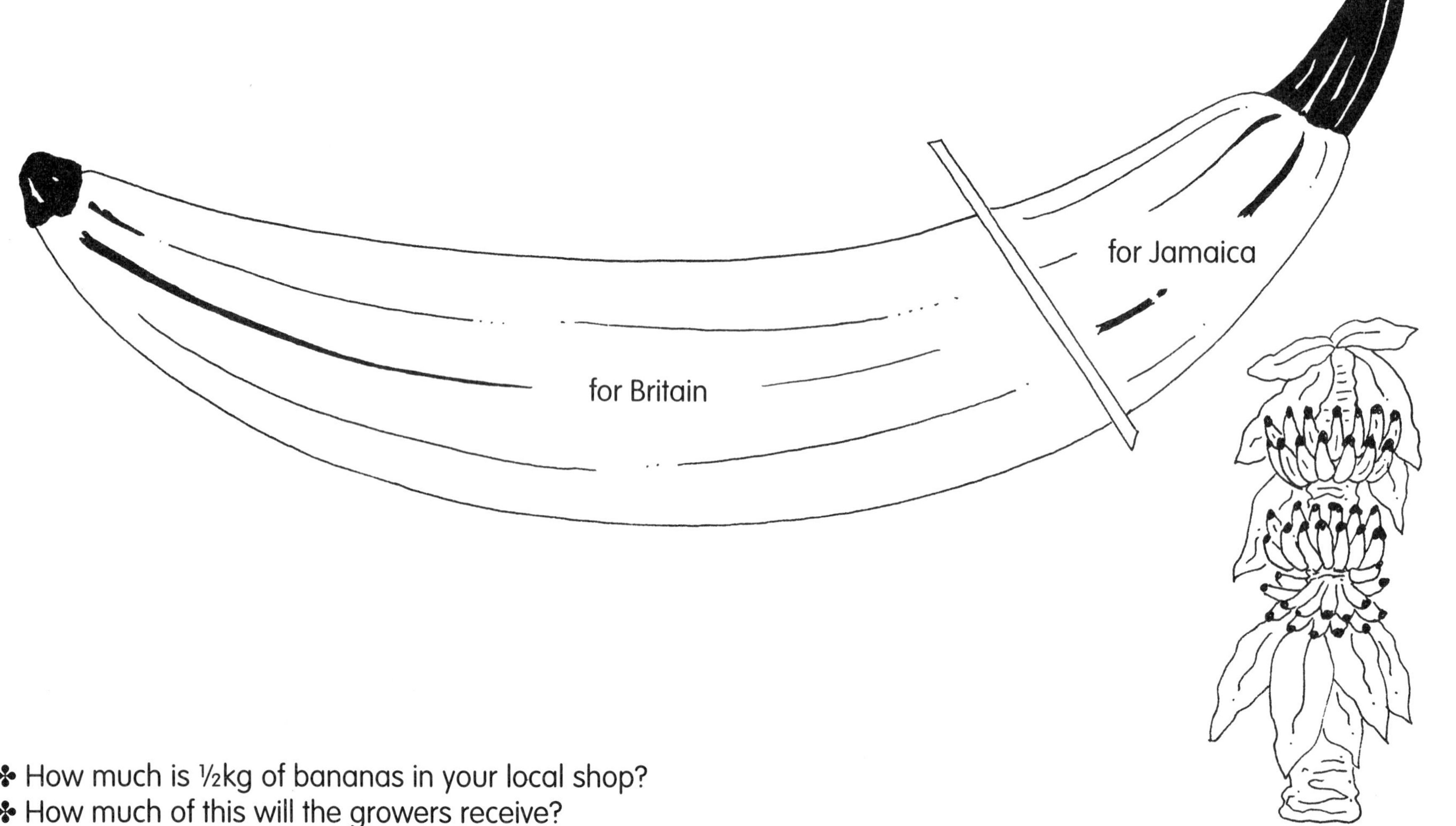

- ✤ How much is ½kg of bananas in your local shop?
- ✤ How much of this will the growers receive?

Name ____________________

Harvest in the city

✤ Write a poem about Harvest in the city.

Name ____________________

Yam Harvest recipe

A yam is a root vegetable grown in West Africa and the Caribbean. In Nigeria there is an annual Yam Harvest celebration.

✤ Try making this yam dish.

What you need

- a yam
- a bowl of cold water
- a saucepan of salted water
- a sharp knife
- butter
- milk

What to do

- Peel the yam and cut it into small pieces. (An adult may need to help you with this part.) When cutting the yam you may see a starchy film on your hands – this will easily wash off. Any decaying parts of the yam should be cut away – the rest will be all right.
- Soak the pieces of yam in cold water for 30 minutes. This will remove some of the sticky film.
- Cook the yam in boiling salted water until tender.
- Drain.
- Mash the yam with butter and milk.

Bread

Below is a collection of different types of bread.

✤ Can you find out the origin for each type of bread?

✤ Why do we connect bread with harvest time?

baguette

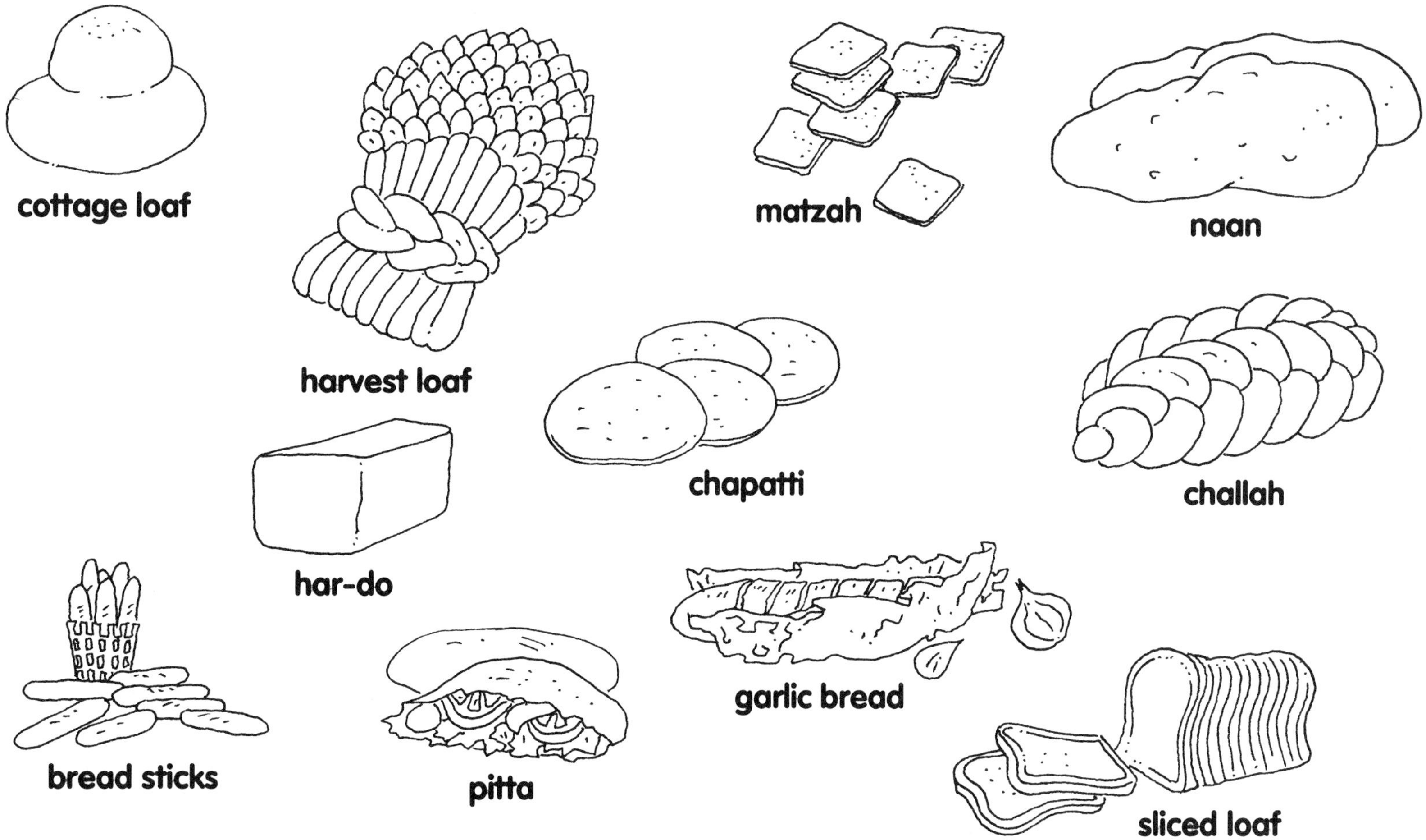

cottage loaf

harvest loaf

matzah

naan

chapatti

challah

har-do

garlic bread

bread sticks

pitta

sliced loaf

Name ____________________

A celebration?

This festival began in America as a day of celebration for the pilgrims' first harvest. It took place at the time of Harvest Home in England. It is thought that the native Americans, under chief Massasoit, taught the pilgrims to hunt, fish and dry and plant corn. Both groups joined together for the original Thanksgiving.

✤ What happened to the original inhabitants of America?

✤ Do you think they still feel like celebrating Thanksgiving?

✤ Write a description or draw a picture/cartoon that will illustrate either what happened to the native Americans or how you would feel if it happened to you.

✤ Now illustrate the story from the point of view of the pilgrims.

Make a sukkah

A sukkah is a temporary shelter which reminds Jews of the time their ancestors spent in the wilderness.

✤ Make your own sukkah.

You will need

- a cardboard box without a lid
- scissors
- pictures of fruit and vegetables
- glue
- doll's house dining room furniture
- twigs with leaves

1 Cut out one side off the box.

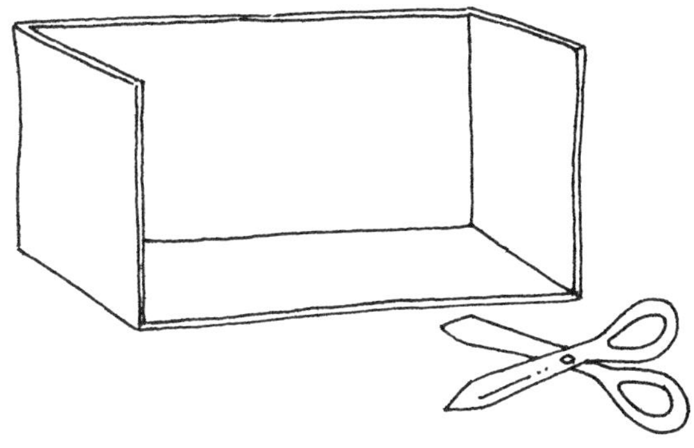

2 Decorate the box, both inside and out, with pictures of fruit and vegetables.

3 Set up the furniture in the sukkah.

4 Spread twigs across the box to form a roof.

Name ____________________

The scroll

✣ Design and make a scroll like the Torah.
These writings are very special to Jewish people.
✣ What would you like to write on a scroll that is special to you?

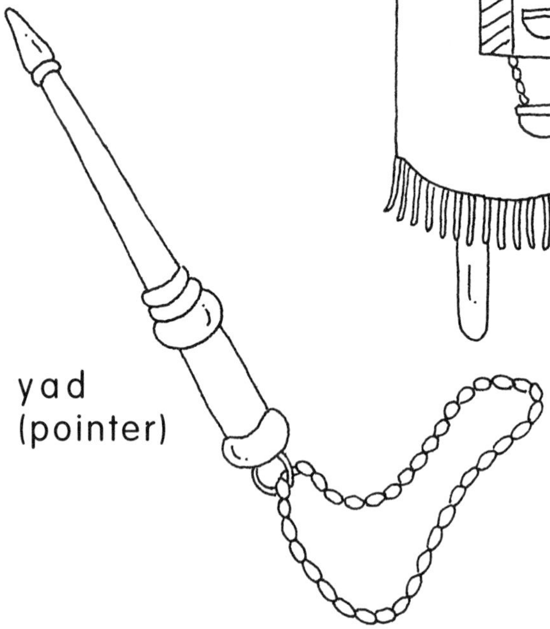

yad
(pointer)

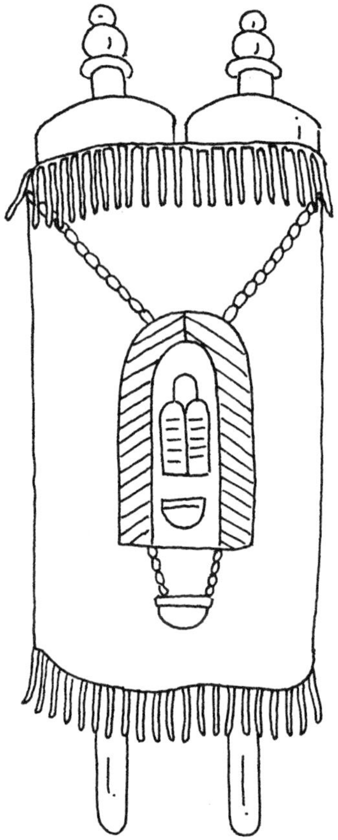

Name ____________________

Design a border

This is a passage taken from the Qur'an (the Islamic Holy Book).

✤ Read it carefully.

'And proclaim the Pilgrimage among men: they will come to thee on foot and [mounted] on every kind of camel, lean on account of journeys through deep and distant mountain ravines'

Qur'an al-Karim, XX11:28

✤ Design a border for this passage that is both geometric and symmetrical.

Name ______________

Buddhist monks

At Kathina new robes are presented to monks.

✤ Find out what you can about life in a Buddhist monastery.

✤ Why do monks dress like this?

✤ Why do they shave their heads?

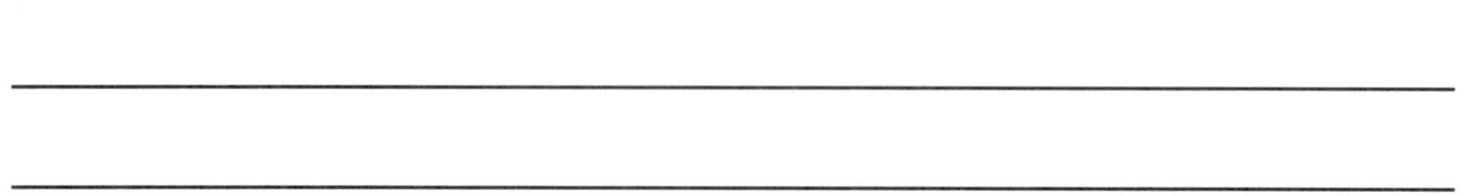

Name ____________________

The story of Rama and Sita

Long ago, in India, King Dasratha ruled over Ayodyha. His eldest son and heir was called Rama. Rama was really the god Vishnu who had taken a human form so that he could rid the world of Ravana, the ten-headed demon.

Queen Kaikeyi was jealous of Rama and wanted her son, Bharat, to be king instead of him. Kaikeyi told so many lies about Rama that eventually Dasratha banished him from his kingdom for fourteen years. Bharat felt that this was wrong and he promised to take care of the kingdom until Rama returned. He put Rama's golden sandals on the throne to show that it was really Rama's.

Rama's wife Sita and his brother Lakshman went with Rama to make a new home in the forest. One day, while the brothers were out hunting, Ravana turned himself into a deer and tricked Sita into moving close to him. As soon as she did, he captured her and took her off to the island of Lanka.

Name ____________________

The story of Rama and Sita (continued)

When Rama and Lakshman returned they searched everywhere for Sita. The monkey king, Hanuman, offered to help them search. The monkeys looked in everywhere and eventually they discovered where she had been taken.

After many adventures they arrived at the sea. The brothers could see no way to cross it, but the monkeys formed themselves into a bridge so that Rama and Lakshman could cross. Ten days of fierce fighting followed, but eventually Rama killed Ravana and rescued Sita.

As soon as the fourteen years were over Rama, Sita and Lakshman left the forest and returned to Ayodhya. People were so happy to see them that they lit divas all over the city. Bharat then removed the sandals from the throne so that Rama and Sita could take their rightful places.

This story is told in the Ramayana and is remembered at Divali each year when Hindus light divas just as the people of Ayodhya did to welcome Rama.

Name ____________________

Cartoon shuffle

✤ Tell the story of Rama and Sita in words and pictures. Cut out the cards and mix them up. See if your friend can put them in the right order.

King Dasratha banished his son, Rama, from his kingdom.

Name ______________

Account book

Divali is a time when business people check that their books are in order.

✤ Keep a record of your income and expenditure for a week. Does it balance?

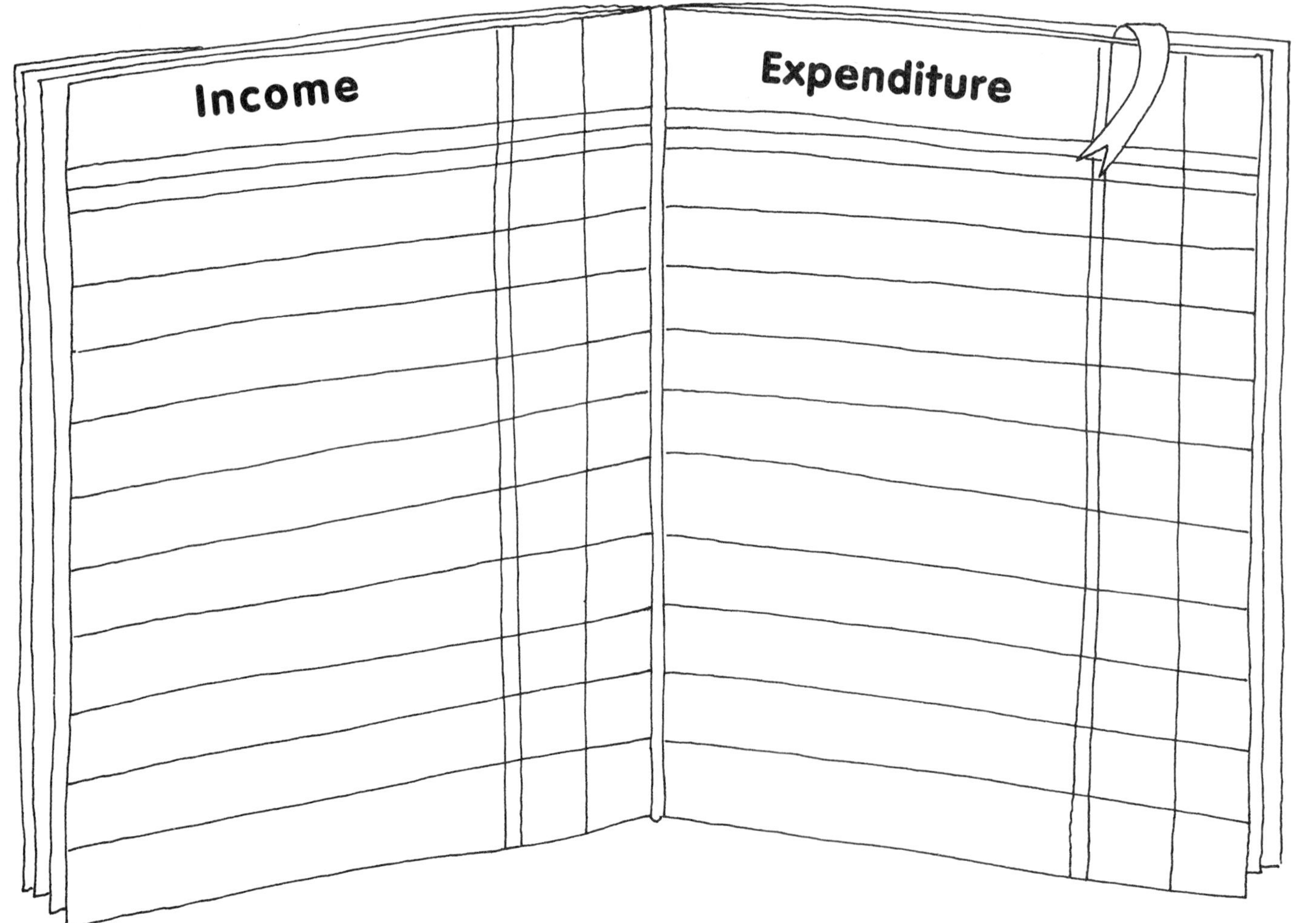

Happy Divali

All of these say the same thing in different languages.

✤ Use them to make decorations.

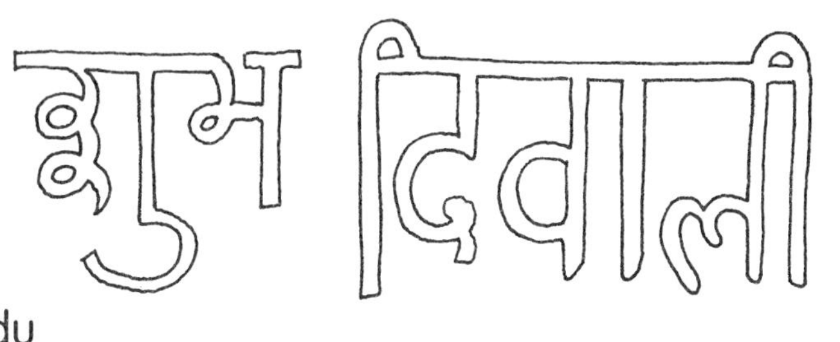

Hindu

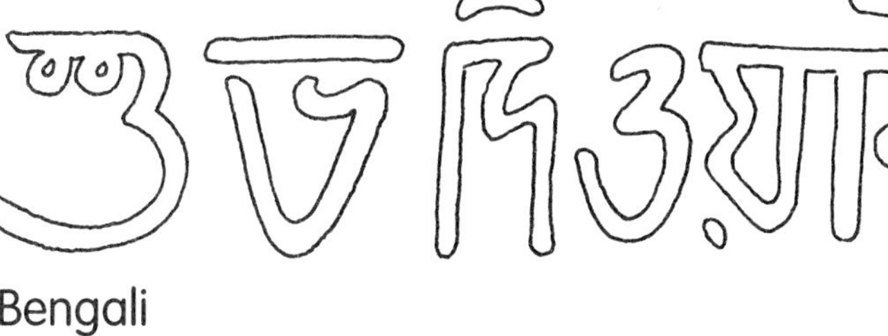

Bengali

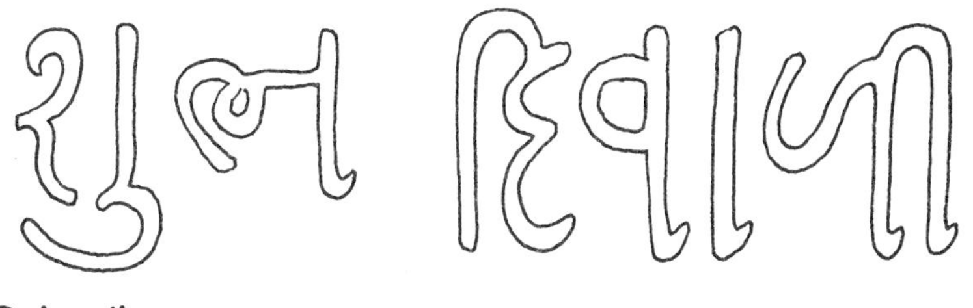

Gujerati

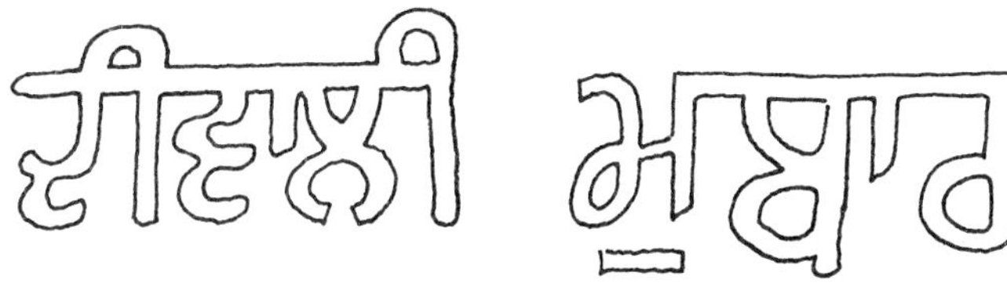

Panjabi

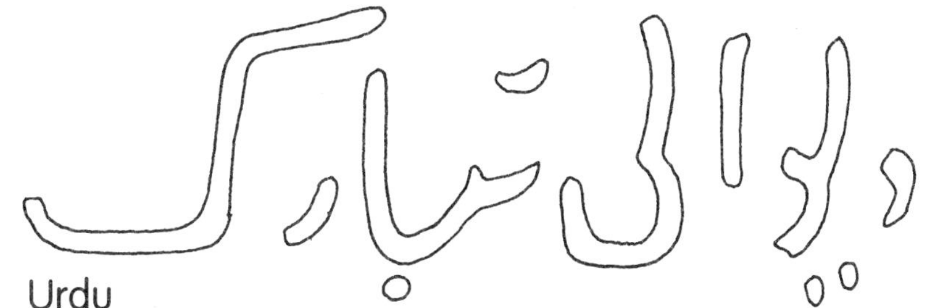

Urdu

Happy Divali

English

Name ____________________

Rangoli patterns

Rangoli patterns are floor patterns which are filled in with coloured powders.

✤ Use the grid on the right to design your own pattern.

Remember that there are at least two axes of symmetry.

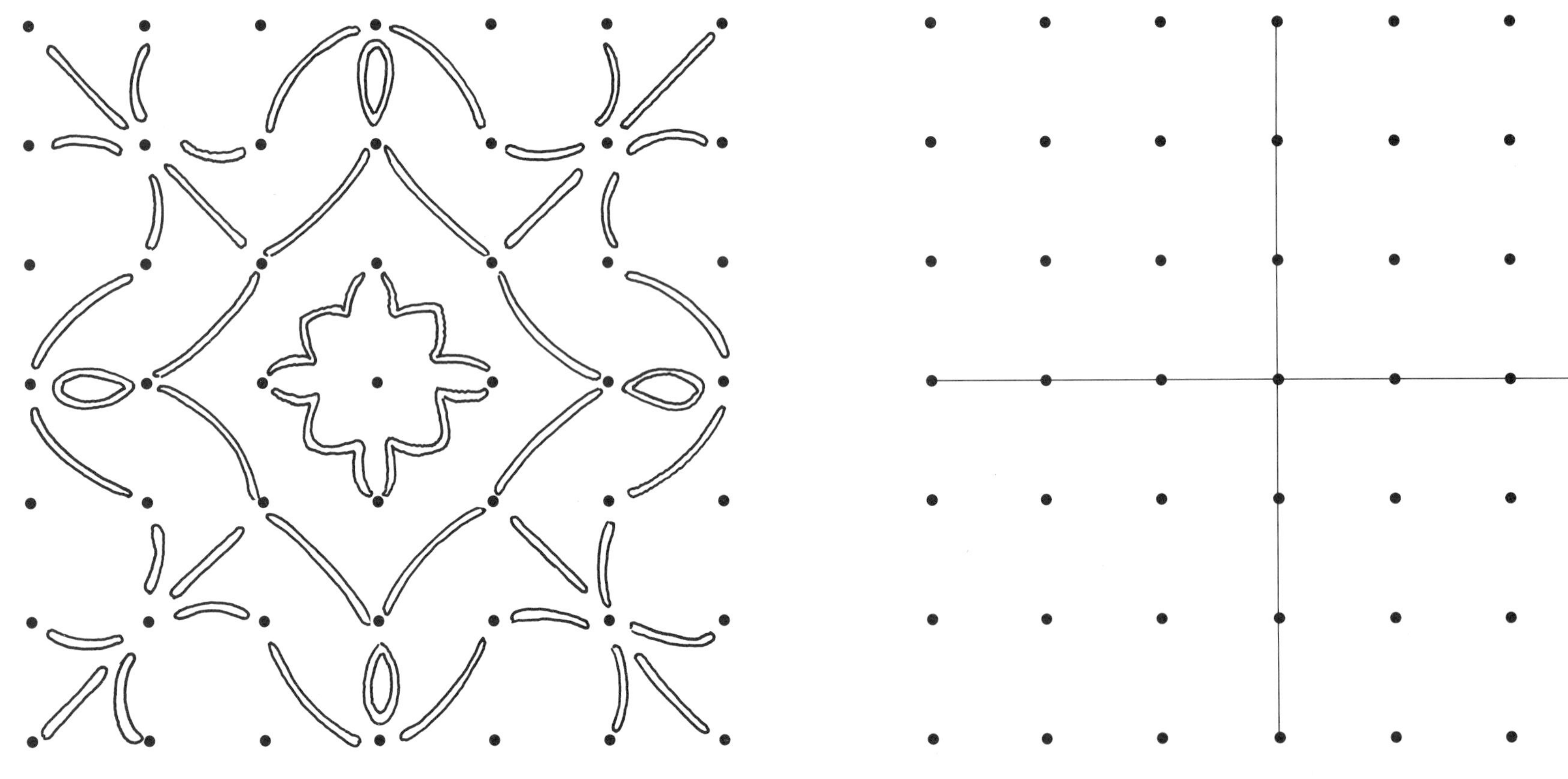

Name ____________________

Mehndi patterns

Henna is used to create patterns on hands (and sometimes feet) during many Indian celebrations. Since henna is a dye the patterns last for several weeks.

✤ Create your own designs below using crayons or washable felt-tipped pens.

Name ____________________

Rama

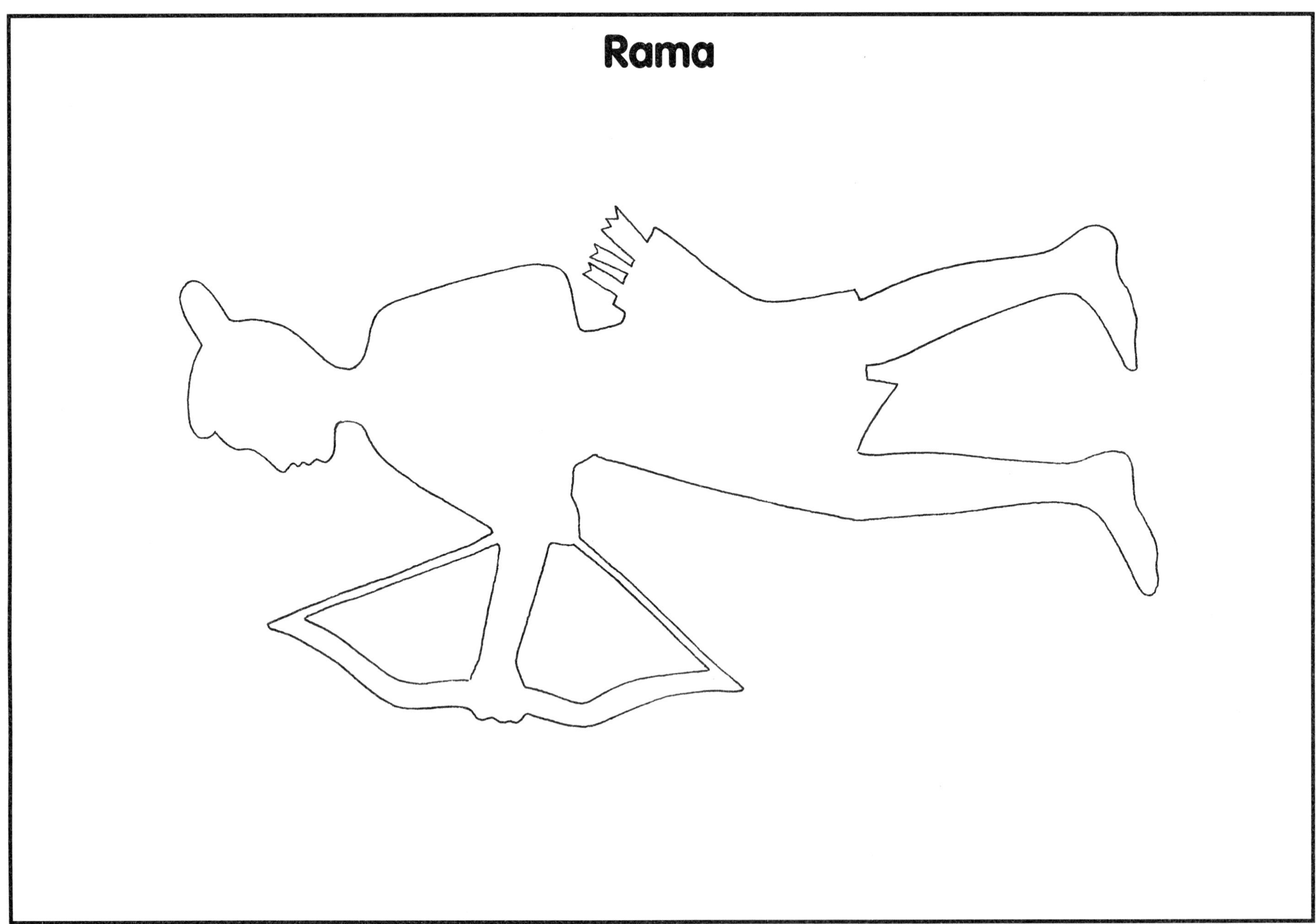

Sita

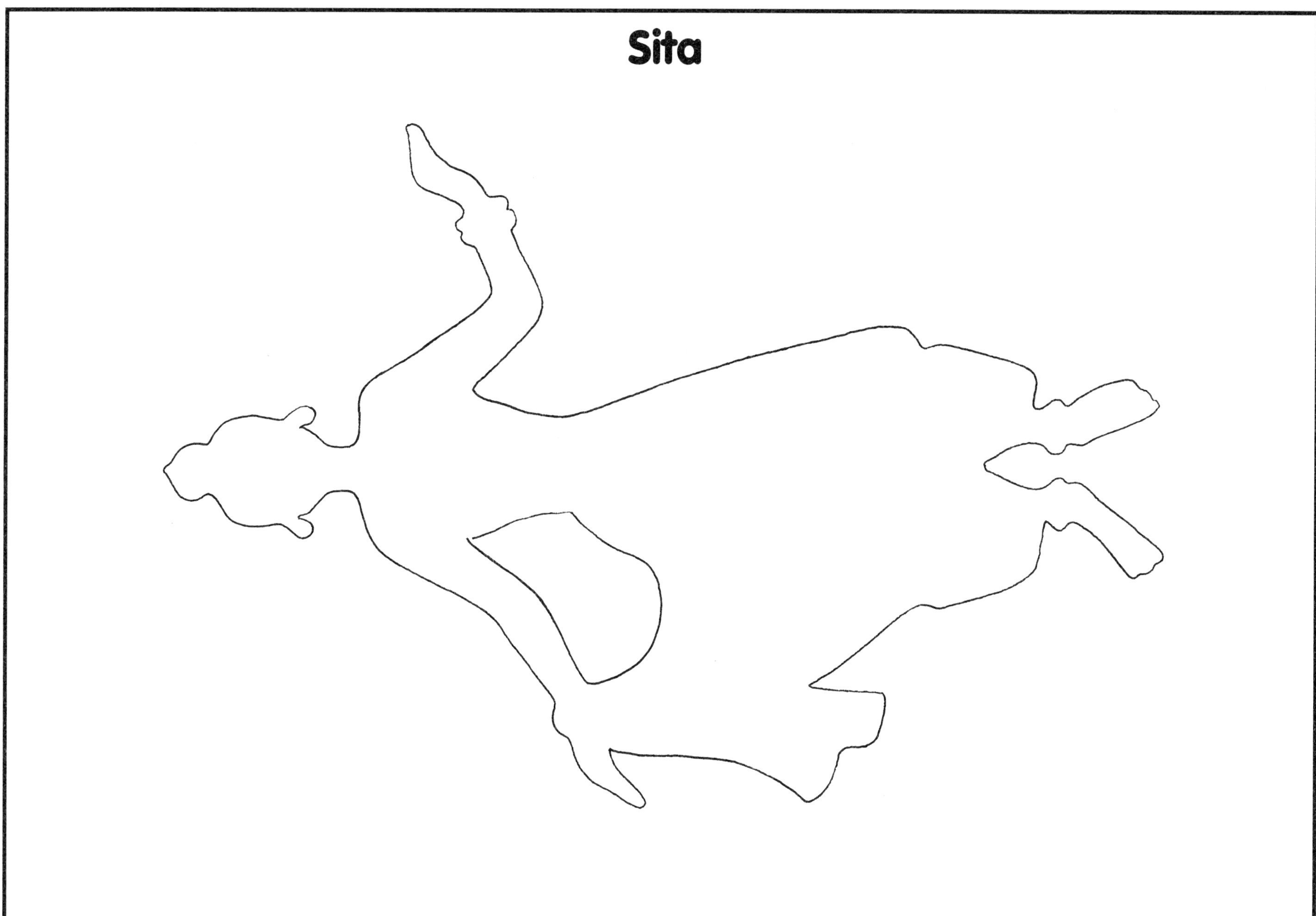

Name ______________

Bharat

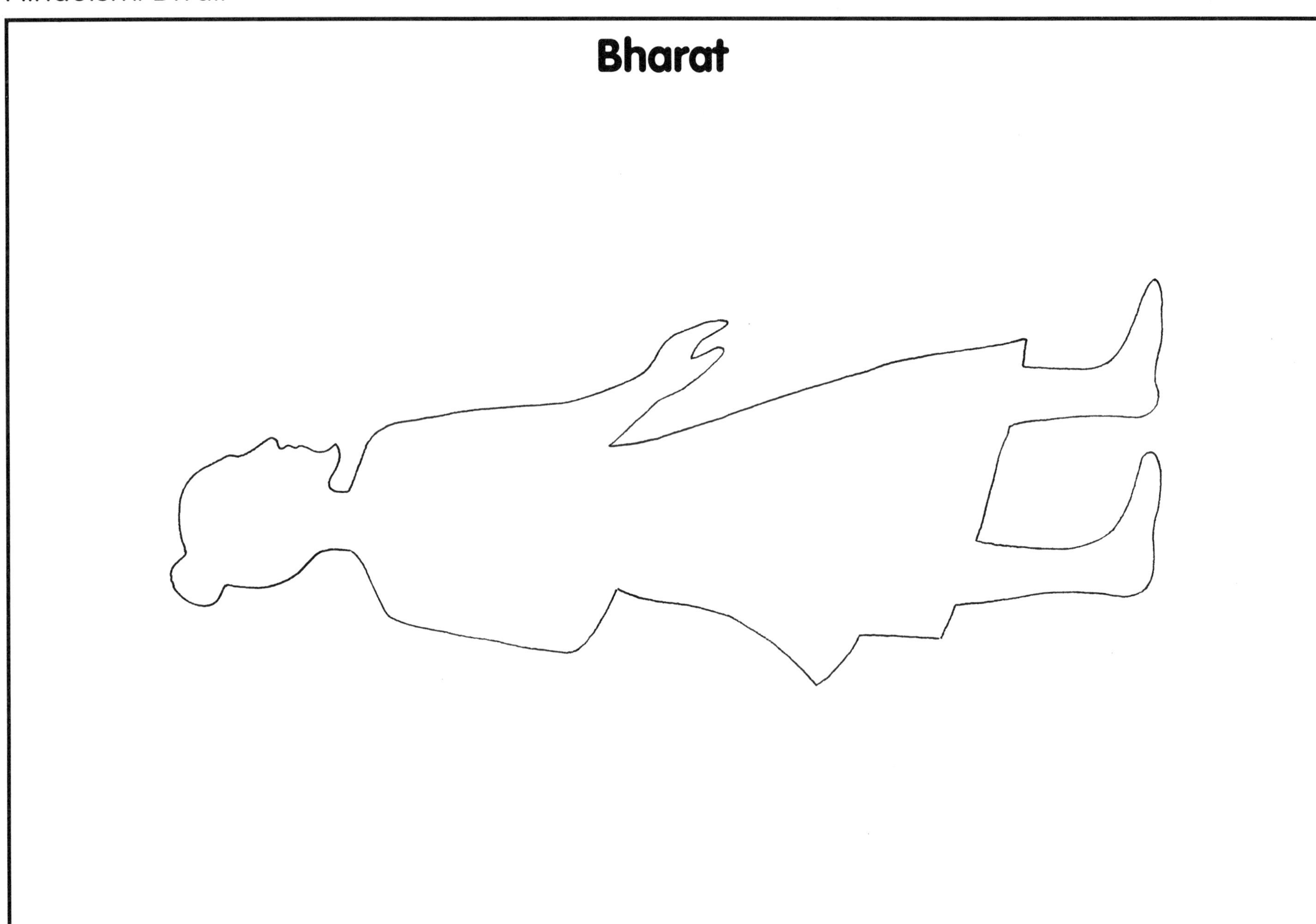

Name ____________________

Ravana

Name ________________

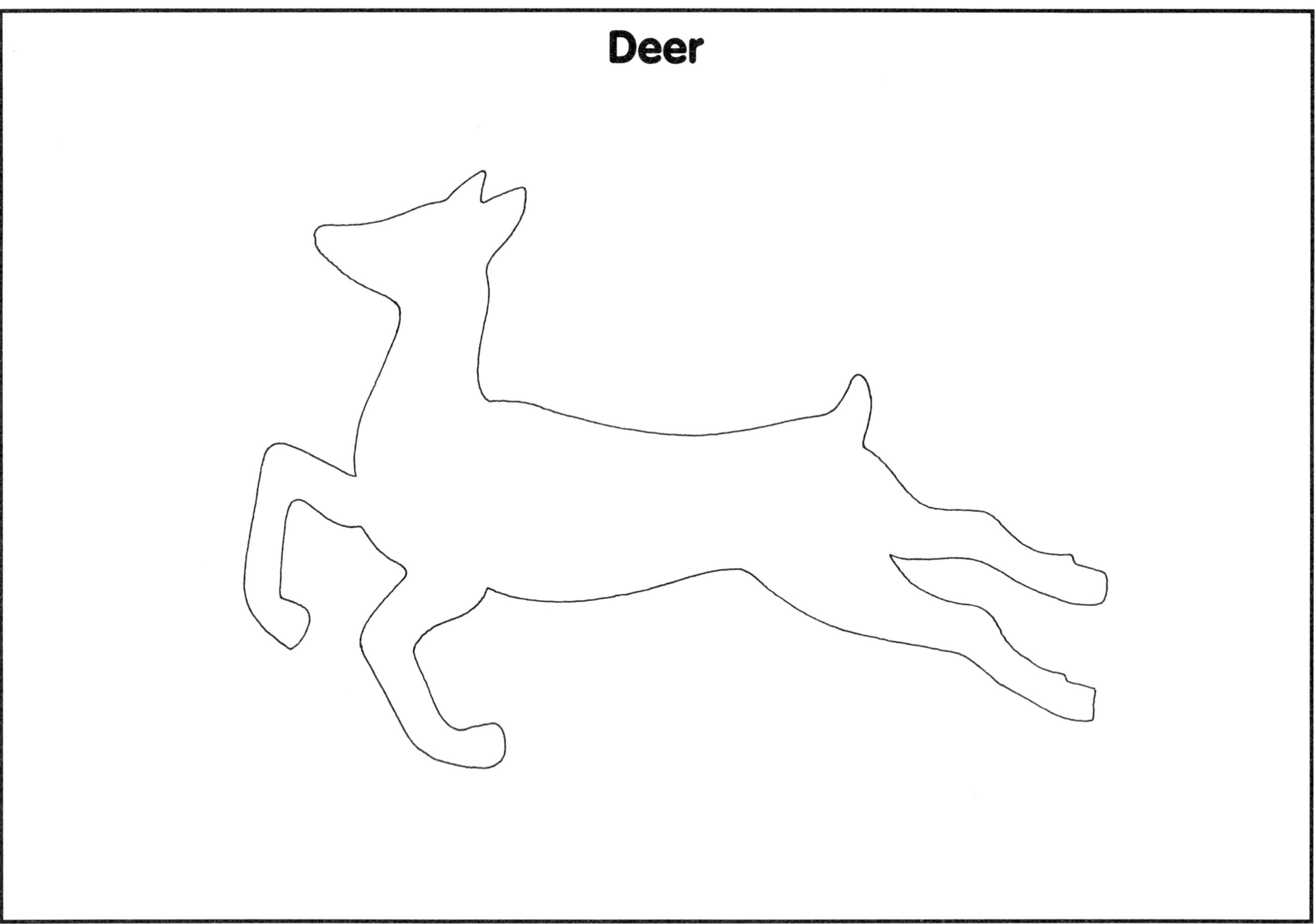

Name ____________________

Hanuman

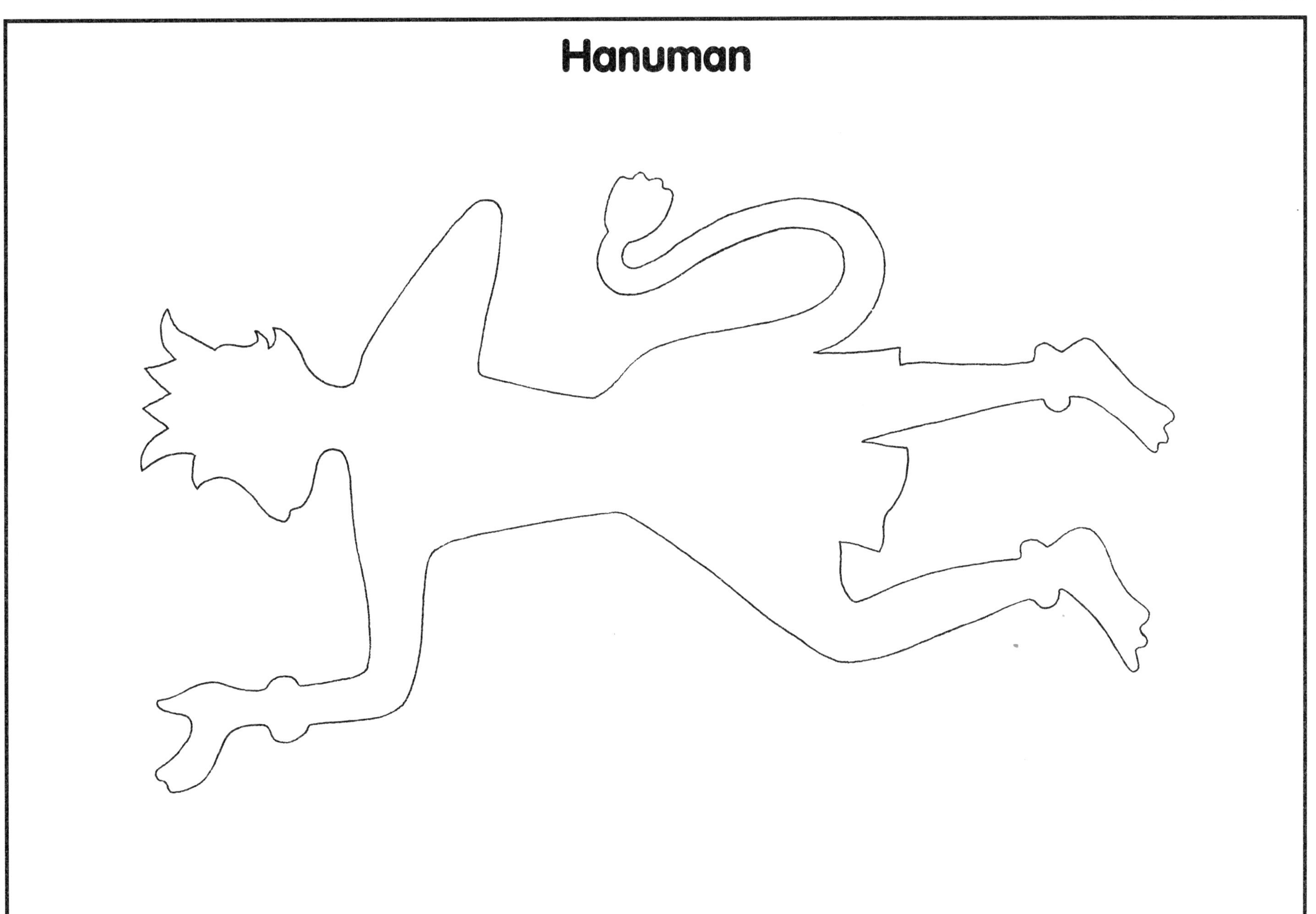

Name ____________________

Clay divas

✤ Sequence the pictures and then make the lamps from clay or a similar material. You can make up your own decorative pattern.

Name ____________________

Greetings card

✤ Design a bright and colourful Divali card.

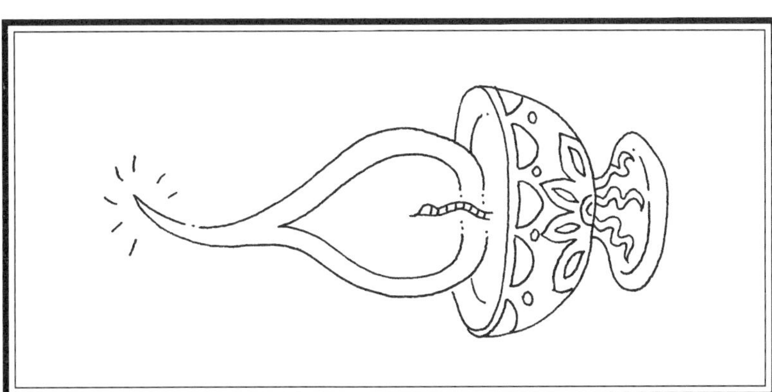

Happy Divali

✤ Experiment with different materials and designs to see which you like best.

Name ____________

The story of the cloak

✤ Illustrate this story

Hargobind became the sixth Guru in 1606 after his father, Guru Arjan, had been tortured to death by the Moguls. Hargobind was only 11 years old at the time, but he became extremely powerful and many Muslims converted to Sikhism. This annoyed the Muslim Governor who resented his popularity. He arrested Guru Hargobind for plotting against the Emperor and imprisoned him, along with 52 Hindu princes, at Gwalior Fort.

Two years later Guru Hargobind was released, but he refused to leave the prison unless the Hindu princes were allowed to leave with him. However, the Emperor said that only those who could hold on to the Guru's clothing as he walked through a narrow passageway would be set free. The Guru therefore ordered a special cloak to be made. It had long tassles on it and the princes were able to hold on to them as the Guru went through the passageway. This way they were all set free. Guru Hargobind immediately returned to Amritsar where his pathway was lit with candles to welcome him.

To remember this day Sikhs celebrate Divali with lights and fireworks. People often visit the gurdwara.

Name ____________________

Happy Divali

✤ Design a card for a Sikh friend.

Name ____________

Modern saints

Gregory was a wealthy Roman who gave his money to help the poor. He became pope and wrote books which told the clergy how to carry out their work, and invented a way of singing the services which became known as the Gregorian Chant. He also sent Augustine to Britain to convert the English to Christianity.

Sybil Phoenix may be thought of as a modern day saint. She is a black woman who has suffered much pain because of her colour, but she is also a woman who has achieved greatness through her tireless voluntary work with young people and her love and dedication to God.

Do you think she will be made a saint?

St Gregory was made a saint partly because of his work with the poor.

✤ Do you know of anyone who could be thought of as a modern saint? Write their story and share it with your class.

____

____

____

____

____

____

____

____

____

____

____

____

✤ Find out about heroes from different faiths.

Name ____________________

The journeys of Guru Nanak

During his life Guru Nanak made many journeys. He visited Tibet, Sri Lanka, Mekka and Bangladesh.

✤ Use an atlas to find the places visited by Guru Nanak. This sketch map will help you.

✤ Mark the Punjab on the sketch map. The Punjab is the district of India where Guru Nanak lived.

✤ Mark the city of Mekka.

✤ Colour the countries visited by Guru Nanak.

✤ What do you notice about the directions in which Guru Nanak travelled from the Punjab?

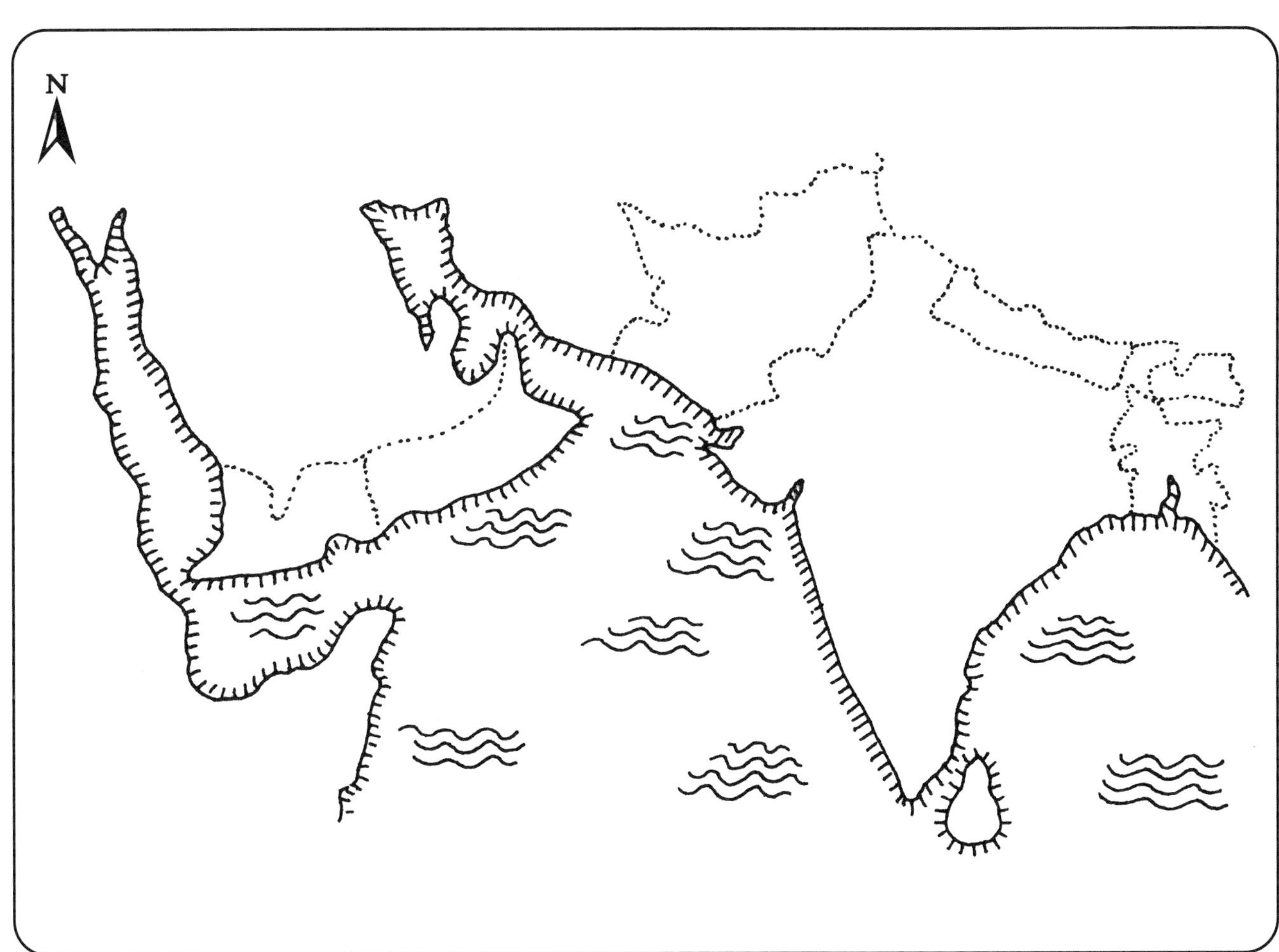

Name ________________

Rastafarian word search

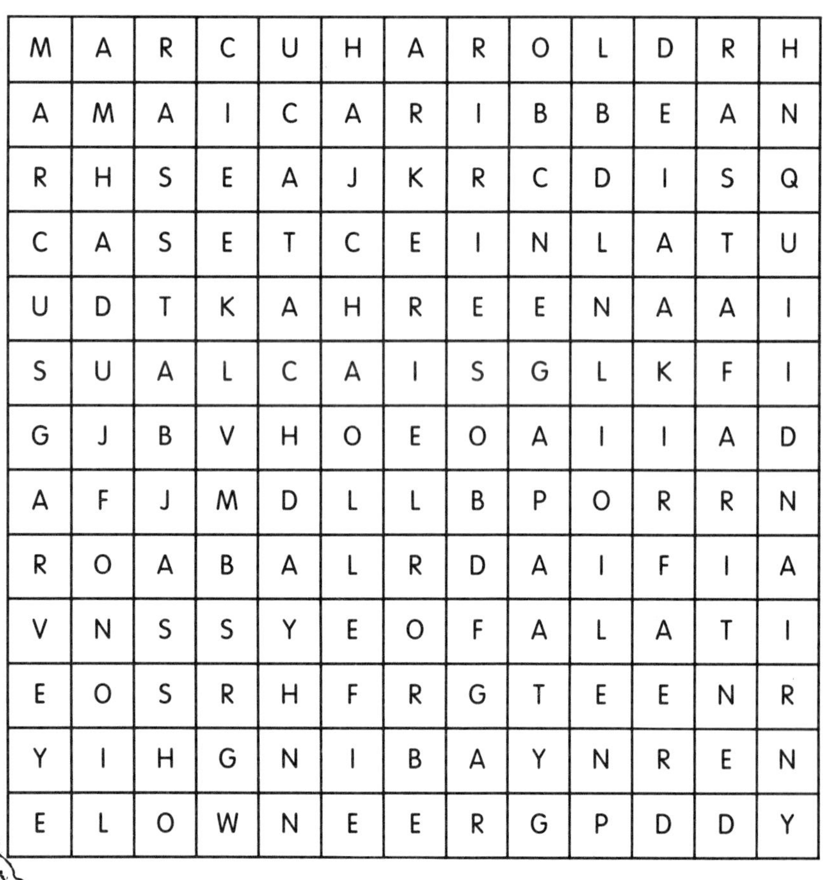

M	A	R	C	U	H	A	R	O	L	D	R	H
A	M	A	I	C	A	R	I	B	B	E	A	N
R	H	S	E	A	J	K	R	C	D	I	S	Q
C	A	S	E	T	C	E	I	N	L	A	T	U
U	D	T	K	A	H	R	E	E	N	A	A	I
S	U	A	L	C	A	I	S	G	L	K	F	I
G	J	B	V	H	O	E	O	A	I	I	A	D
A	F	J	M	D	L	L	B	P	O	R	R	N
R	O	A	B	A	L	R	D	A	I	F	I	A
V	N	S	S	Y	E	O	F	A	L	A	T	I
E	O	S	R	H	F	R	G	T	E	E	N	R
Y	I	H	G	N	I	B	A	Y	N	R	E	N
E	L	O	W	N	E	E	R	G	P	D	D	Y

✤ Complete the word search and then find out what these words mean to a Rastafarian.

red	Haile Selassie
Jah	Lion of Judah
Ital	Marcus Garvey
gold	dreadlocks
green	Ras Tafari
black	Caribbean
herbal	Nyabinghi
Afrika	Ethiopia
I and I	Amharic

✤ Design a border for your word search using the Rastafarian colours of black, red, green and gold.

Name ____________________

St Andrew's Day assembly

Name ______________

Floating lights

During this festival boats are made from leaves and used to float candles across a river.

✤ Can you design a leaf-boat that is able to carry a candle?

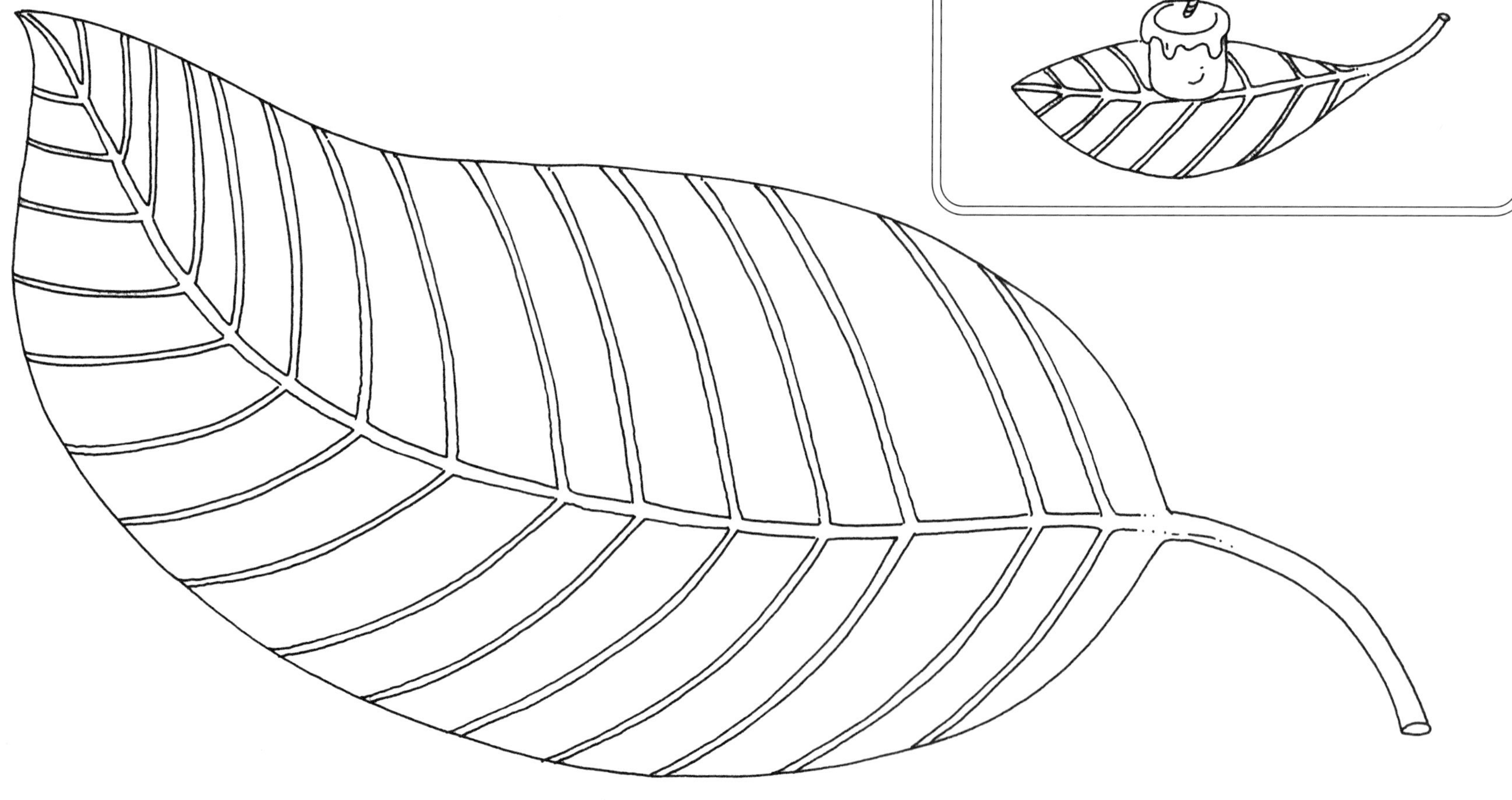

Friendship

✤ Think about a special friendship. Write about what makes that friendship so special.

Name ____________________

Advent candle

✤ Colour the decoration at the base of the candle.
Colour one mark on the candle every day during December.
The flame will be coloured in on Christmas Day.

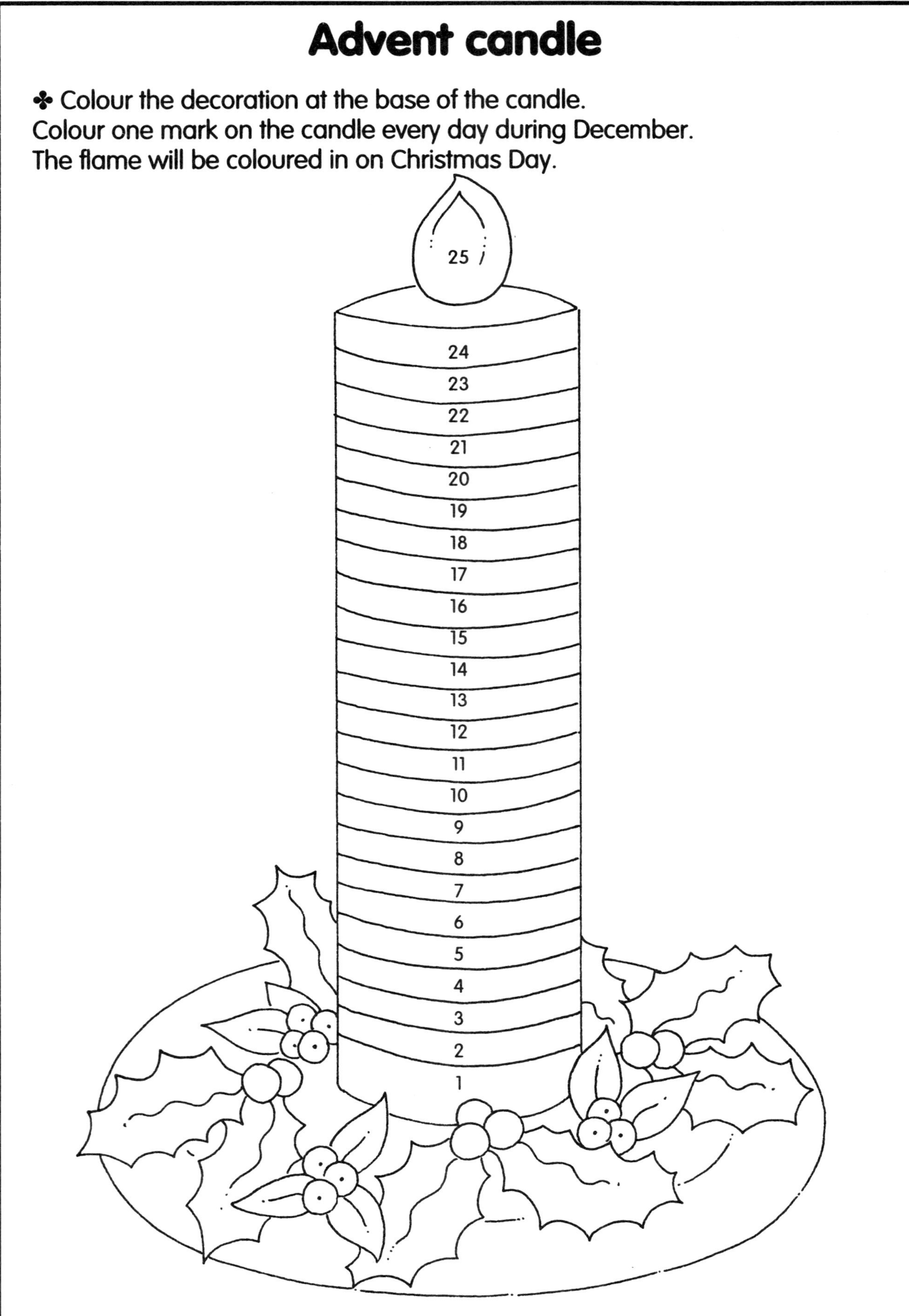

Hanukah dedication

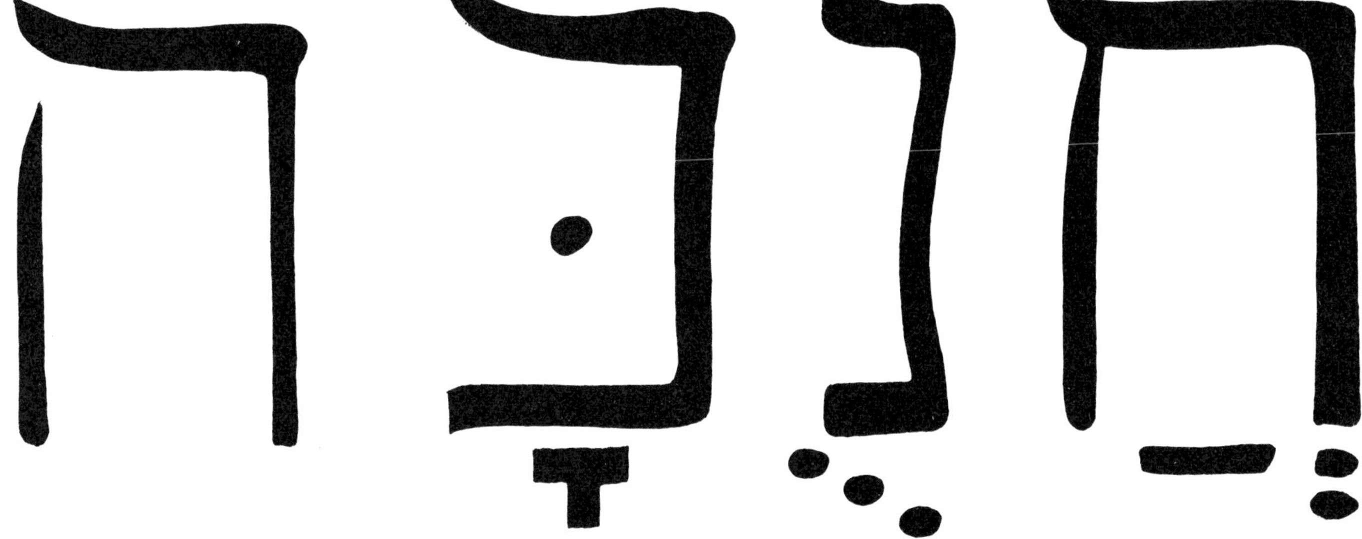

Name ____________________

The story behind Hanukah

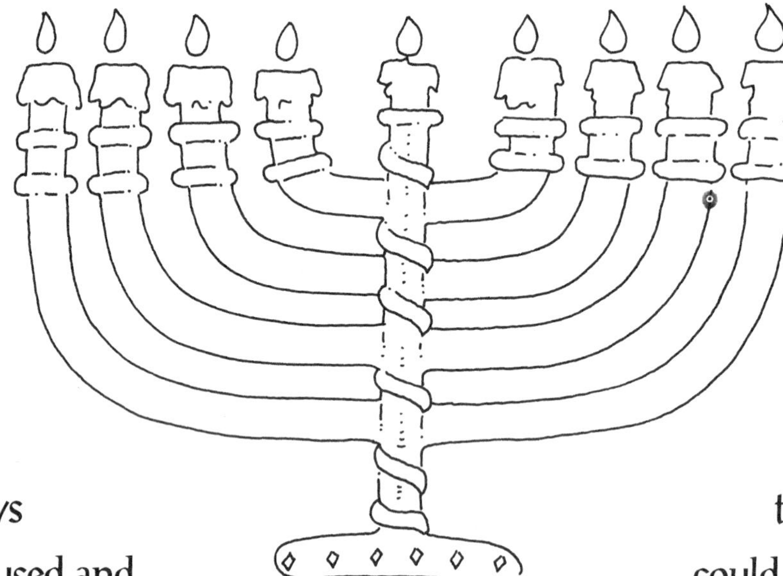

Over 2000 years ago the Jewish people were ruled by the king of Syria. They were allowed to worship as they wanted until the wicked Antiochus became king. He believed in the Greek religion and wanted the Jews to follow him. The Jews refused and Antiochus was extremely angry. He ordered his soldiers to march into Jerusalem. They killed hundreds of Jews and they ransacked the temple stealing the special menorah from the altar. They then used the temple for playing games and feasting. The Jews were unable to use it for prayer and they were frightened of the soldiers and afraid of what else might happen to them.

Mattathias persuaded the Jews that they should fight back. He told them that it might take a long time, but he believed that they could win. He, his sons and friends hid in caves behind Jerusalem. They would attack the enemy unexpectedly and retreat to their hiding places. They were not trained soldiers but were extremely brave. Mattathias was old and when he died his son, Judah the Maccabee, became leader. Judah promised that they would

The story behind Hanukah (continued)

not rest until the menorah was burning in the temple again.

The battles went on for over two years by which time there was very little food, water or oil left in the city. Judah and his followers stormed the city and finally drove out the enemy. The Jews were free again. They were delighted and immediately began to restore the temple.

When they came to light the menorah they discovered that there was only enough oil to last for one day. They prayed that it would last until they were able to get some more oil and the flames burned for eight days. If anything they were even brighter than before.

From that time onwards Jews have remembered these eight special days with a festival of lights. The word 'Hanukah' means 'dedication' and the holiday celebrates the rededication of the temple.

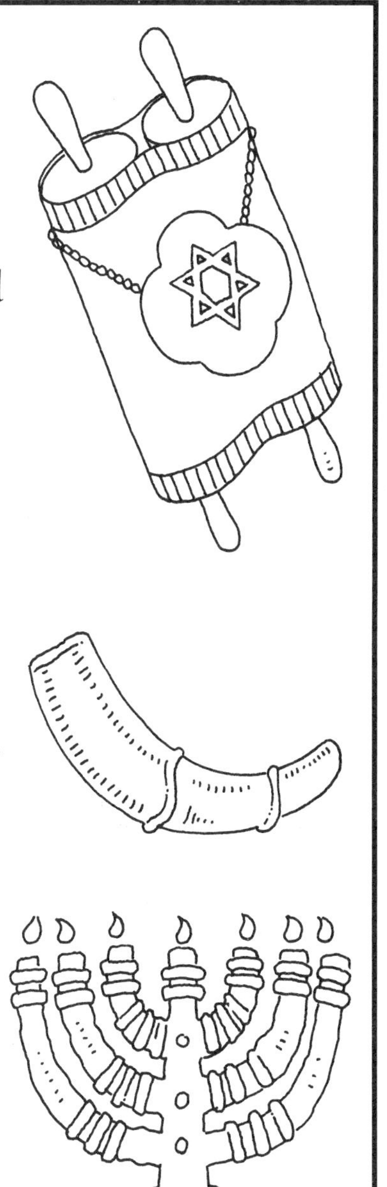

Name ____________________

Happy Hanukah

✤ Design your own Hanukah card.

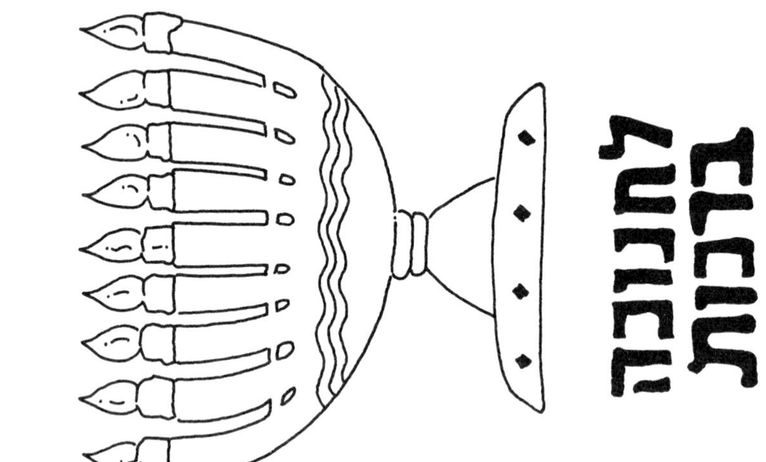

HAPPY
HANUKAH

Make a dreidel

✤ Cut out the template below and use it to make a dreidel.

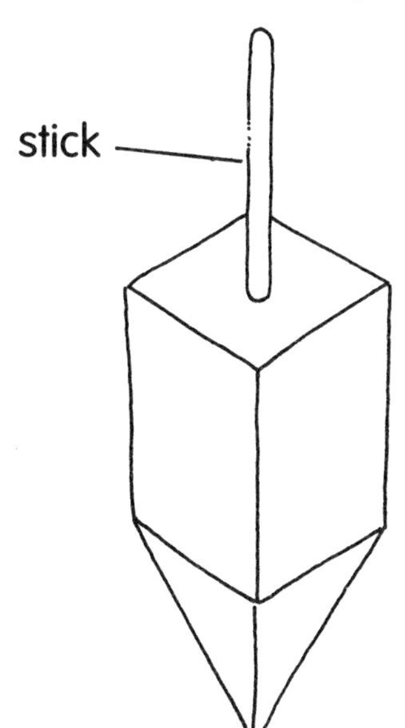

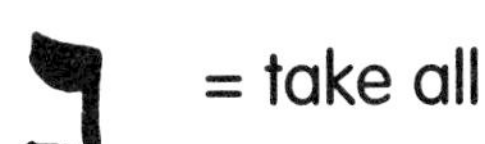

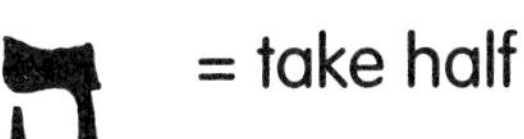

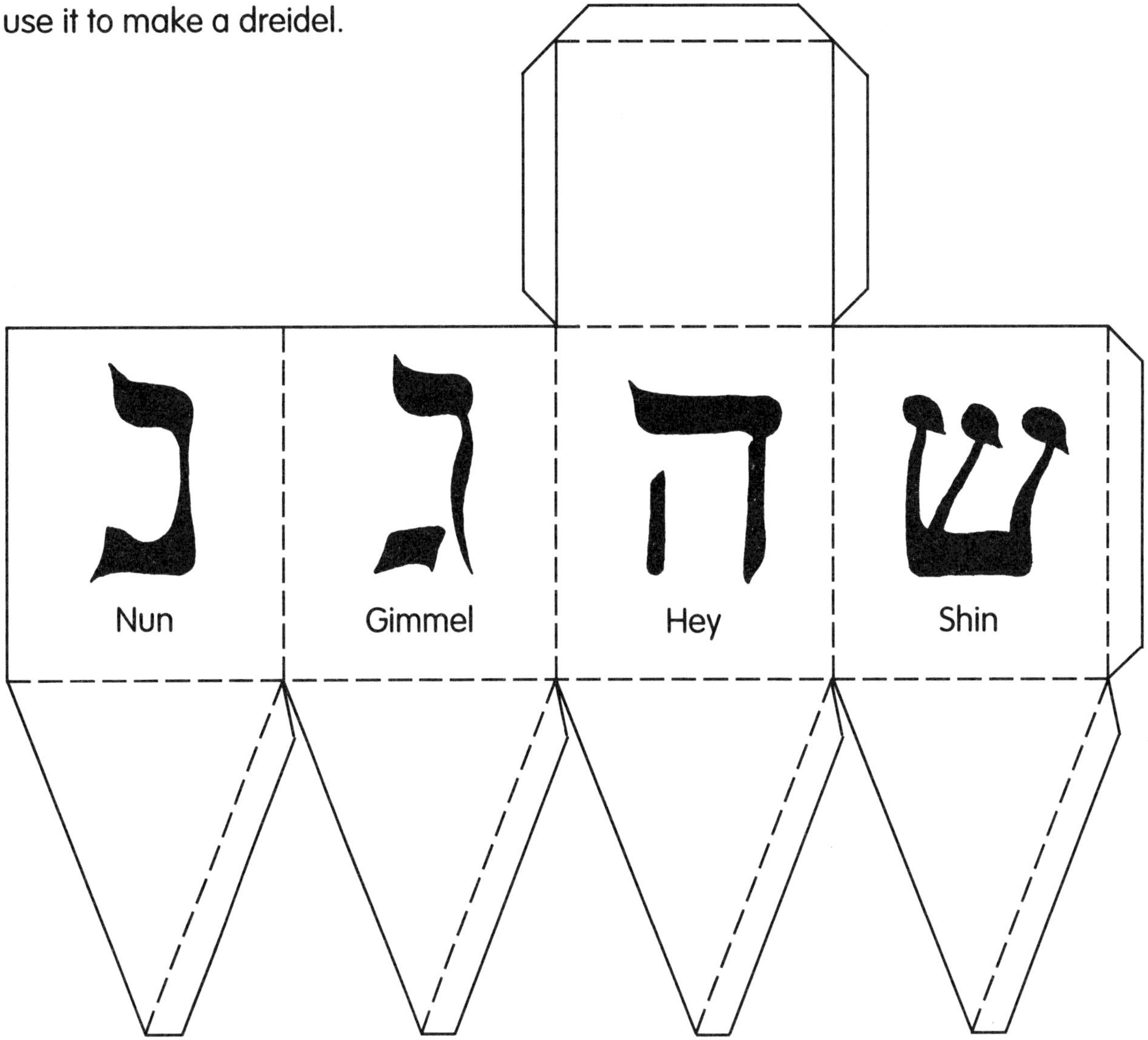

נ	ג	ה	ש
Nun	Gimmel	Hey	Shin

Name ______________

Make a menorah

Menorahs like the one shown below can be made out of many materials such as clay and Plasticine.

✤ Work in pairs to design and make a menorah.

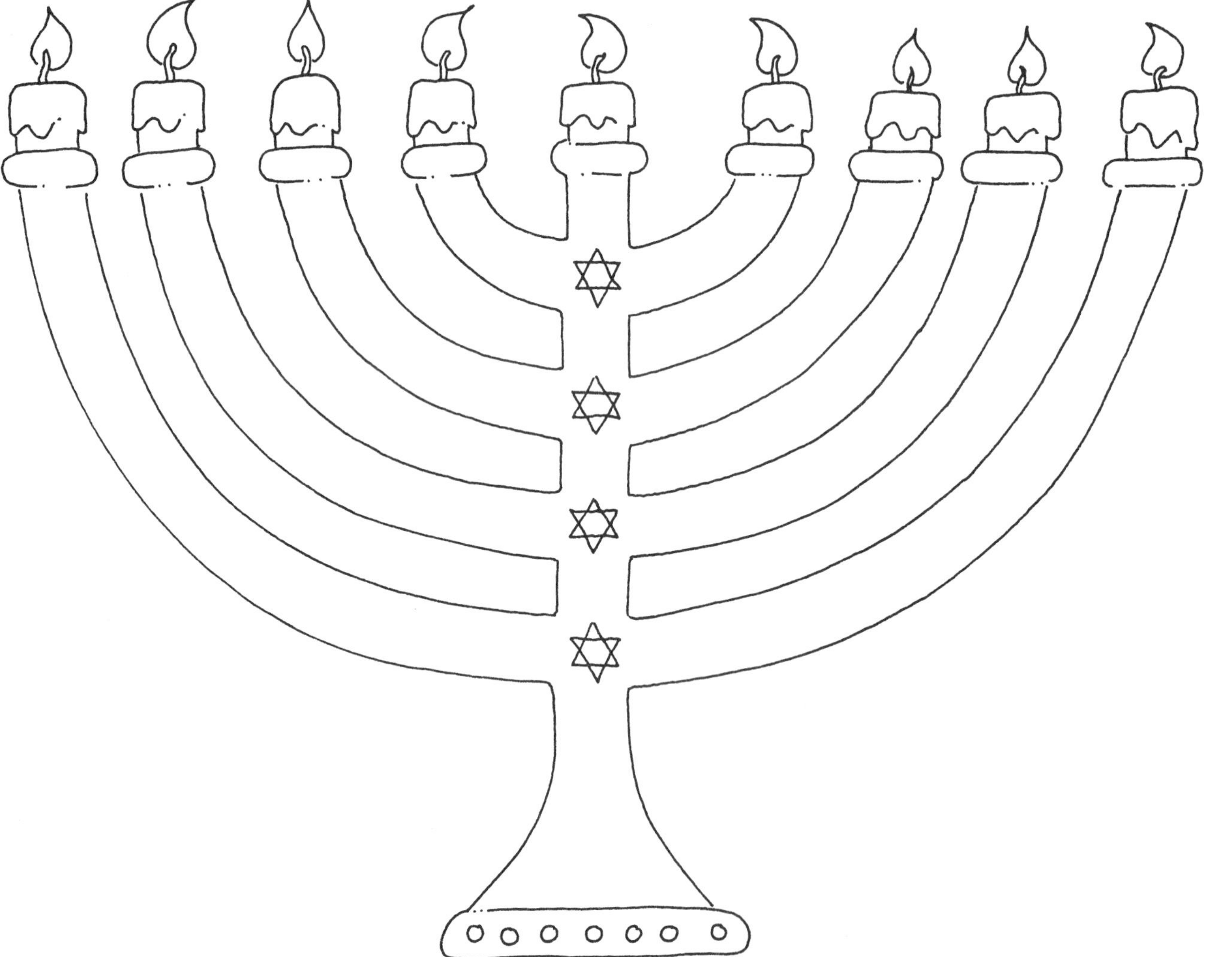

Name ___________________

Potato latkes

Potato latkes are traditionally eaten at Hanukah. Frying them in oil is a reminder of the miracle of the jug of oil.

What you need

- 3 large potatoes (peeled)
- a small onion
- 2 eggs
- 2 tablespoons flour
- 1 teaspoon salt
- oil for frying
- mixing bowls
- grater
- frying pan
- mixing spoons

What to do

- Grate the potatoes into a bowl.
- Grate in the onion.
- Add eggs, flour and salt and mix together until smooth.

SAFETY: YOU NEED AN ADULT TO HELP WITH THIS

- Heat the oil in the frying pan.
- Drop spoonfuls of the mixture into the hot oil.
- Fry on both sides until cooked.
- Serve with apple sauce.

Name ____________________

Christingle

Each object in a Christingle is used as a symbol and has its own meaning.

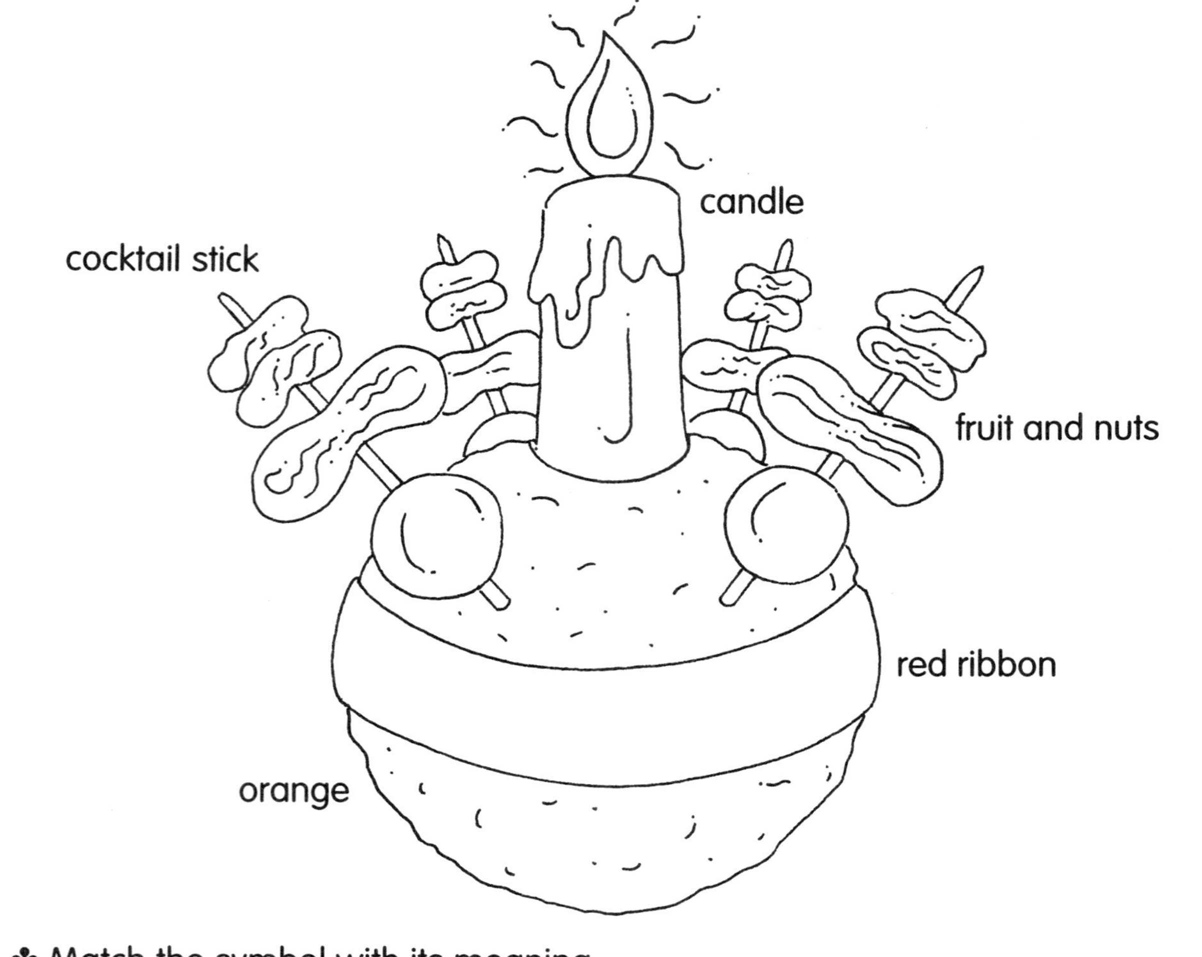

✤ Match the symbol with its meaning.

Orange	The fruits of the earth
Candle	The blood of Christ
Red ribbon	The world
4 cocktail sticks	The light of the world
Nuts and dried fruits	The four seasons

Name ____________

What happened next?

✤ Continue the Nativity story in words and pictures.

There was no room at the inn.

Name ____________________

Christmas stamps

The first 'Christmas stamp' was issued in Canada in 1898.

✤ If you had the choice, what would you draw on a Christmas stamp? Draw some below.

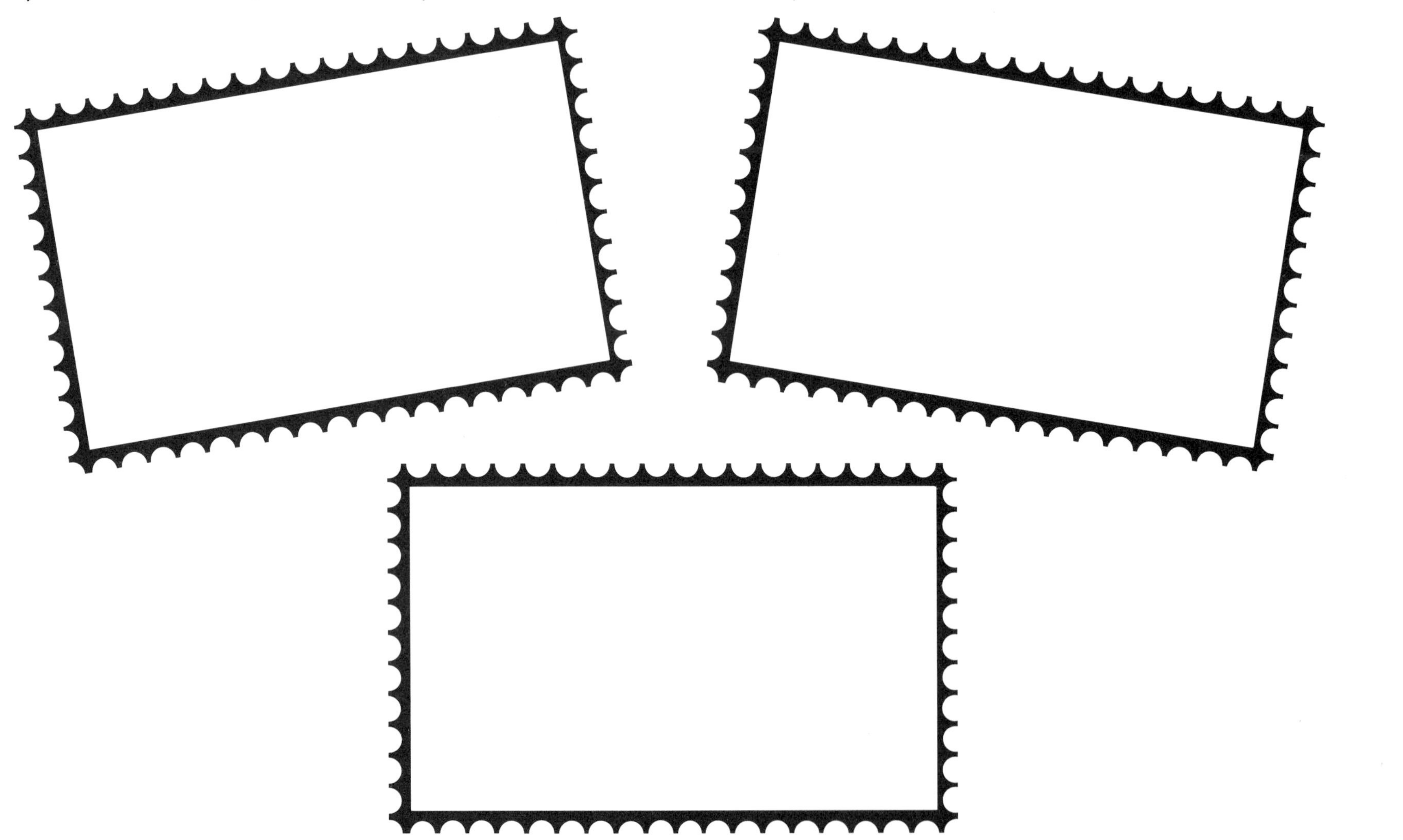

Christmas letter

✤ Write to a friend describing how you are going to spend Christmas.

Name ______________

Poinsettia

This traditional Christmas plant is found growing in Mexico and the Caribbean.

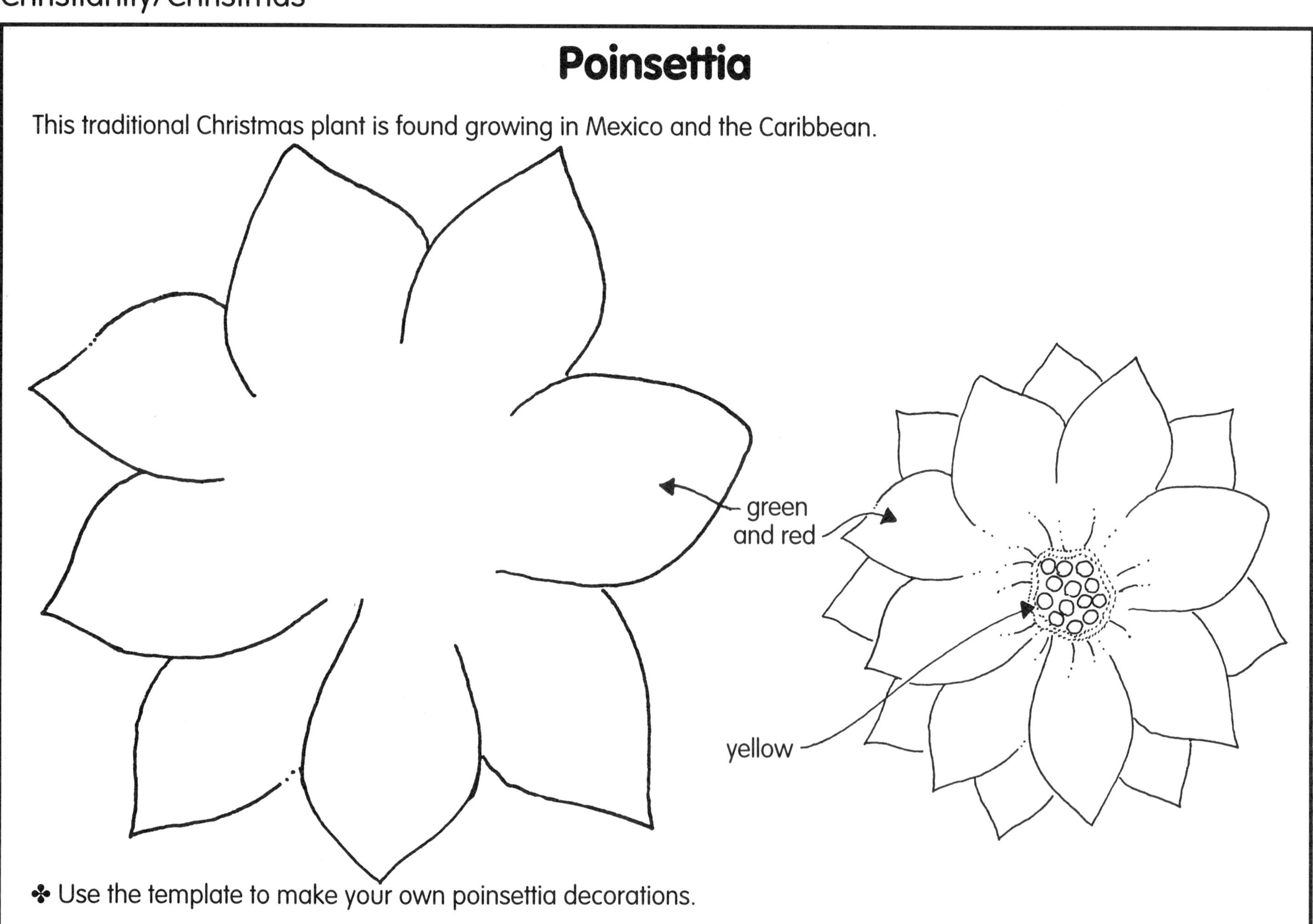

✤ Use the template to make your own poinsettia decorations.

Christmas greetings

✤ Use these greetings inside your Christmas cards or as part of a wall display.

Wesołych Świąt

Polish

Feliz Navidad

Spanish

Urdu

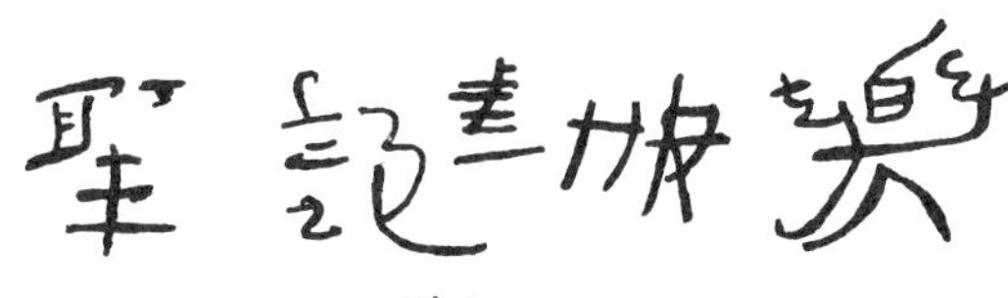

Chinese

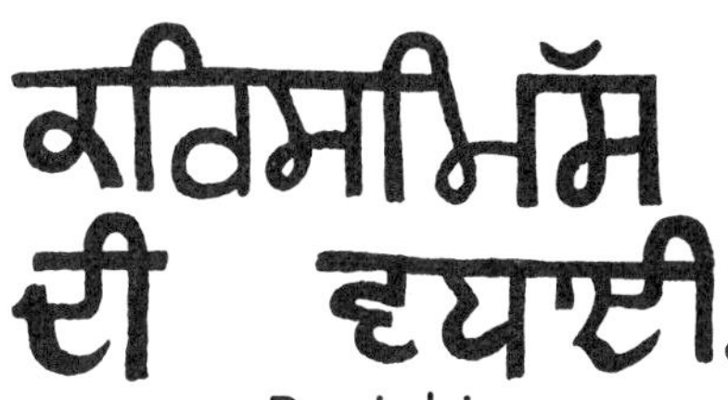

Panjabi

Happy Christmas

English

Nadolig Llawen

Welsh

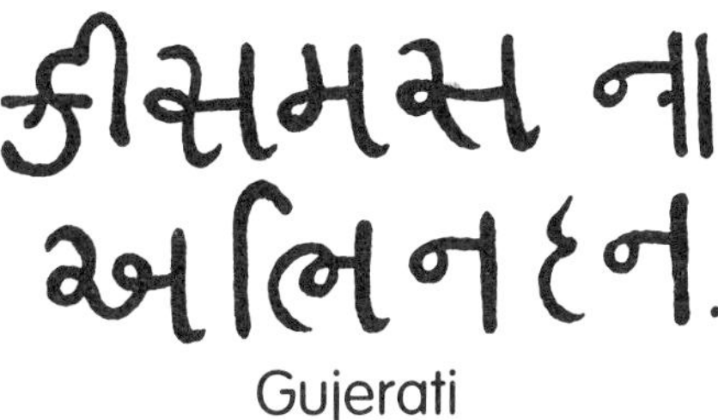

Gujerati

क्रिसमस
की
बधाई

Hindi

শুভ খ্রীষ্টমাস.

Bengali

Nollaig shona duit

Irish

Buon Natale

Italian

Name ____________________

'Auld lang syne'

✤ Find out what this poem means and illustrate it.

Should auld acquaintance be forgot.
And never brought to mind?
Should auld acquaintance be forgot,
And days of auld lang syne.

For auld lang syne, my dear,
For auld lang syne,
We'll tak' a cup o' kindness yet,
For the sake of auld lang syne.

By Robert Burns

Name ________________

My New Year resolutions

I will try to...

keep my room tidy

watch less television

stop eating sweets

get more exercise

be kind to my brother

clean my shoes

help with the housework

wash Mum's car

Name ______________

'There is only one race – the human race'

Guru Gobind Singh

Name ____________________

The Three Wise Men

✤ Decorate and cut out this Wise Man.
Fold it into a cone and stick it together at the back.
✤ Make two more and decorate
them differently.

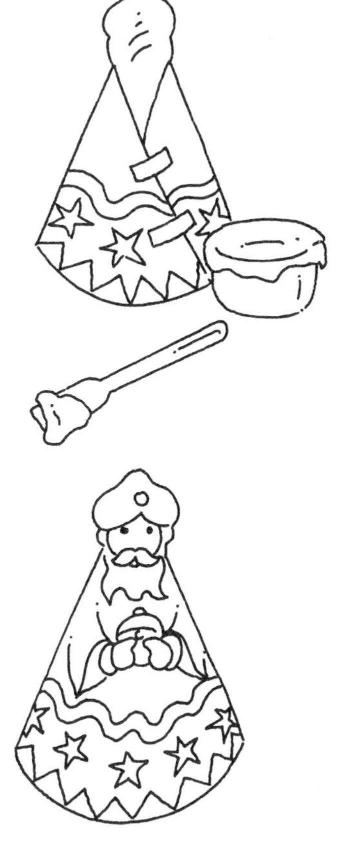

Name ______________

Kite flying

During Basant people in the Punjab (India) make and fly kites (pathana).

✤ Draw a picture of children playing with yellow kites and wearing yellow clothes. Even the adults who are watching will be wearing yellow.

Name ____________________

Saraswati – the goddess of learning and the arts

Name ____________

How the years got their names

A long time ago in China, the gods decided that they wanted to name the years after animals. They chose twelve animals – dragon, tiger, horse, snake, pig, cockerel, rat, rabbit, ram, dog, ox and monkey.

All of these animals wanted the first year to be named after them as they all thought themselves to be the most important. Can you imagine the noise when they were arguing? They made so much noise that they woke up the gods.

After listening to all their arguments the gods decided to settle the matter by holding a race across a wide river. The years would be named according to the order in which the animals finished the race.

How the years got their names (continued)

The animals were very excited. They all believed that they would win – although pig wasn't quite so sure. During the race there were many changes in position, with different animals taking the lead.

As they approached the river bank ox was in the lead with rat a very close second. Rat was determined to win but he was getting very tired. He had to think quickly. He managed to catch ox's tail and from there he climbed on to his back. Ox could see that he was winning but just as he was about to touch the bank, rat jumped over his head and landed on dry land. Can you imagine how ox felt? Rat, of course, was delighted. The other animals agreed that rat had been too clever for the faster ox.

The gods kept their word and named the years after the animals. They began with Rat, then Ox, Tiger, Rabbit, Dragon, Snake, Horse, Ram, Monkey, Cockerel, Dog, and last, but not least, Pig.

✣ Write and act a short play based on this story.

Name ______________

Ordering dominoes

✤ Stick the dominoes on to card then cut along the double lines. You should have twelve cards.
✤ Cut each card into two along the single line.
✤ Mix up all the cards.
✤ Ask a friend to match up the two parts of each card and put the correct cards in order.
✤ How can you make the game easier? How can you make it more difficult?

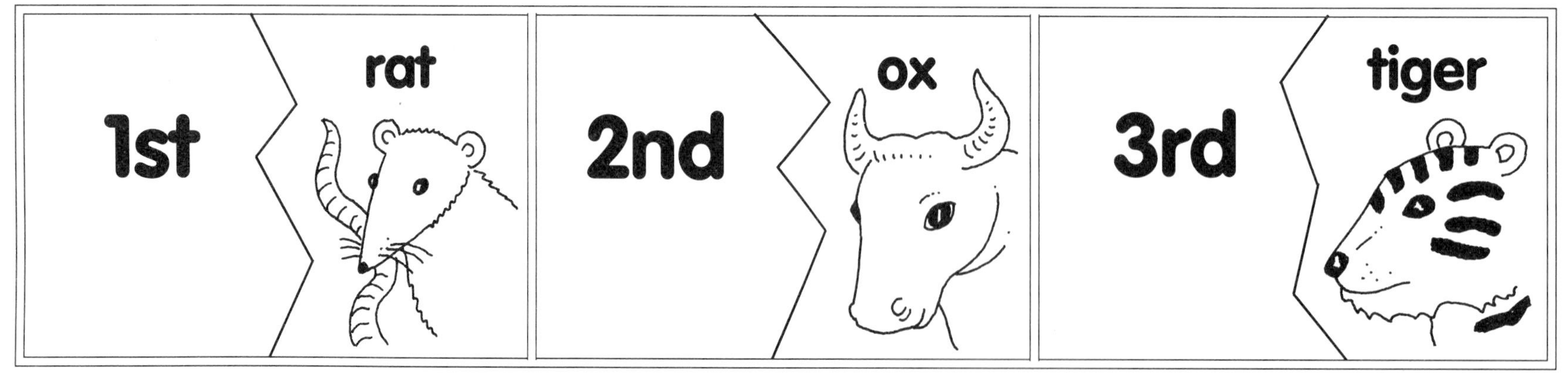

Name ____________________

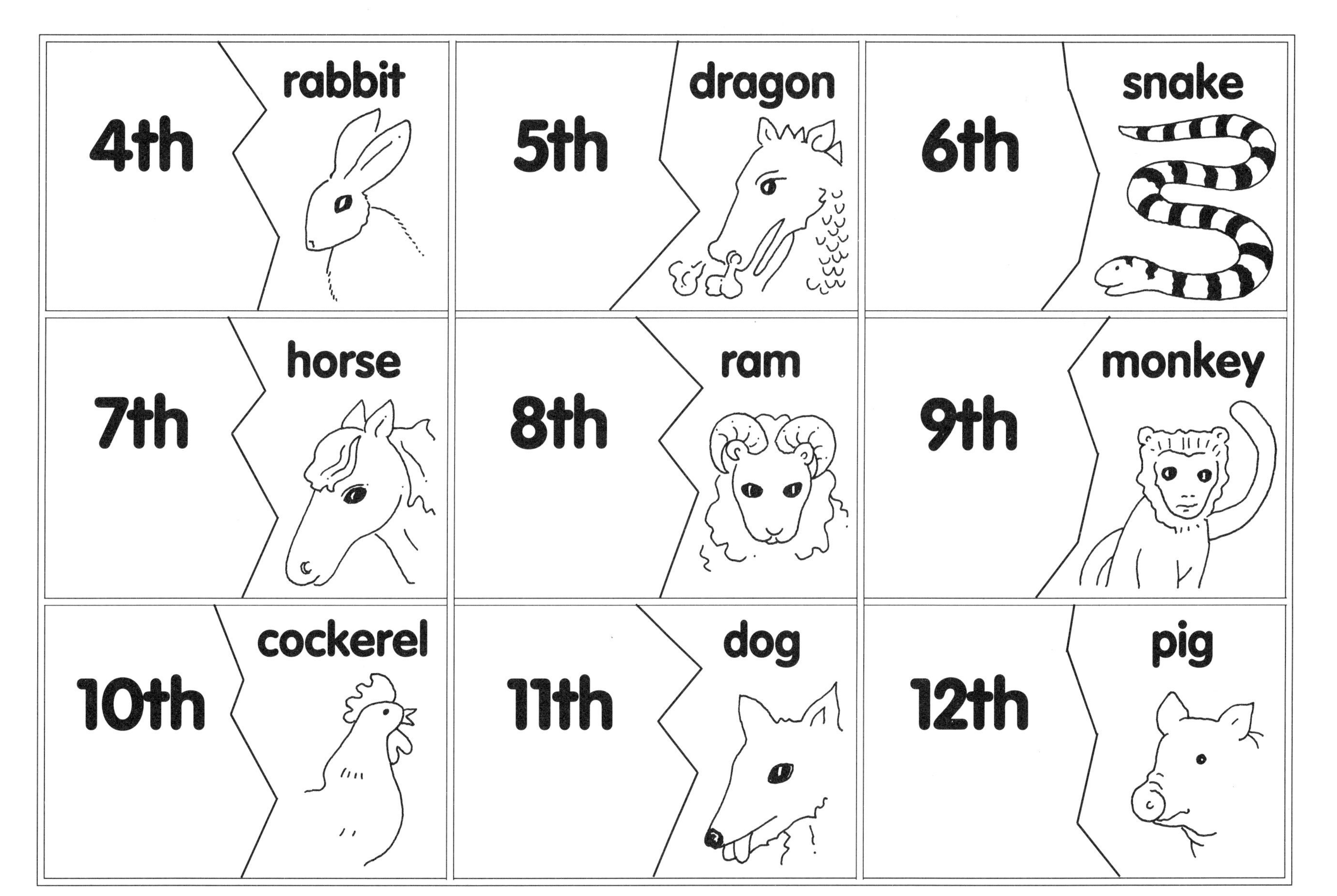
4th
rabbit
5th
dragon
6th
snake
7th
horse
8th
ram
9th
monkey
10th
cockerel
11th
dog
12th
pig

Name ____________________

In which year were you born?

Rat	Ox	Tiger	Rabbit
1924 1936 1948 1960 1972 1984 1996	1925 1937 1949 1961 1973 1985 1997	1926 1938 1950 1962 1974 1986 1998	1927 1939 1951 1963 1975 1987 1999
Dragon	**Snake**	**Horse**	**Ram**
1928 1940 1952 1964 1976 1988 2000	1929 1941 1953 1965 1977 1989 2001	1930 1942 1954 1966 1978 1990 2002	1931 1943 1955 1967 1979 1991 2003
Monkey	**Cockerel**	**Dog**	**Pig**
1932 1944 1956 1968 1980 1992 2004	1933 1945 1957 1969 1981 1993 2005	1934 1946 1958 1970 1982 1994 2006	1935 1947 1959 1971 1983 1995 2007

Chinese horoscopes

✤ Do you know of anyone who matches up to these characteristics?

Rat Charming but quick-tempered. Should have an easy life if born during the day but will have to work hard if born at night.	**Ox** Calm and quiet but stubborn. Should have a happy and successful life.	**Tiger** Usually intelligent and should do well. Tends to be brave, thoughtful and honest, but rather touchy.	**Rabbit** Could be lucky and successful but can be moody. Should have a happy life with several children.
Dragon Tends to be emotional and eccentric. A good leader. Takes life easy and prefers the night-time.	**Snake** Wise and attractive but rather conceited. Works hard. Likely to have a variety of jobs.	**Horse** Cheerful and intelligent. Enjoys doing good. Can be impatient.	**Ram** Timid and indecisive. Can be artistic. Will enjoy helping others.
Monkey Intelligent and curious – finds it difficult to mind own business. Works hard.	**Cockerel** Hard-working and arrogant. Can sometimes appear dreamy.	**Dog** Can be selfish but is generally loyal and honest. Makes a good friend.	**Pig** Takes things easy. A bit of a spendthrift. Intelligent. Often a good parent but can get angry easily.

Name ______________

Blossom tree

The blossom tree is a symbol of good luck.
✤ Make one as a decoration.

What you need

- a yoghurt pot
- paper to decorate the pot
- twigs
- sand
- glue
- pink tissue paper circles

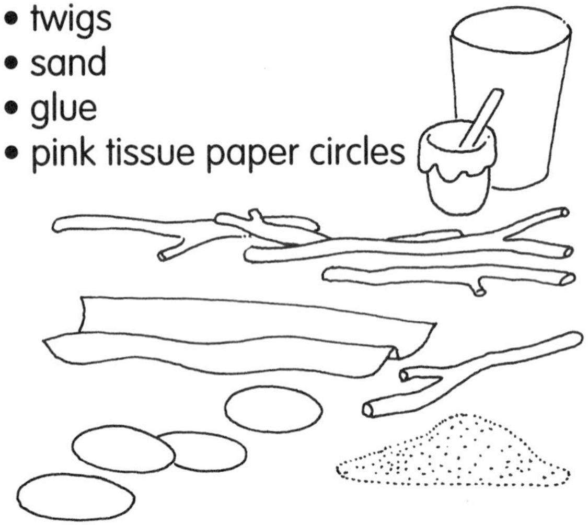

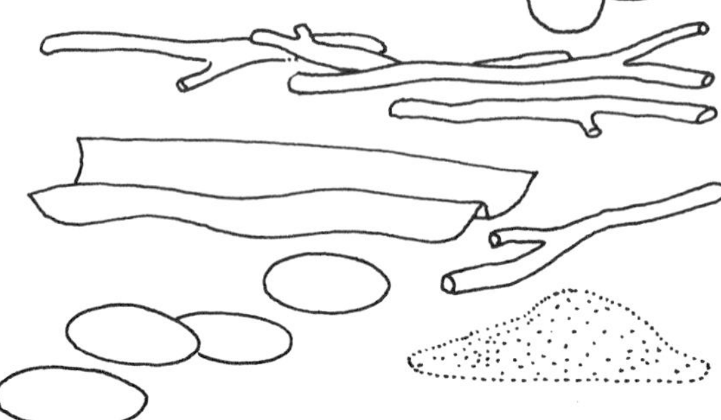

What to do

- Decorate the yoghurt pot with paper.
- Fill the pot with sand and stand the twig in the pot.
- Pinch the centre of the tissue paper circles and twist them to form flowers.
- Glue the flowers on to the twig.

Name ____________________

HAPPY NEW YEAR

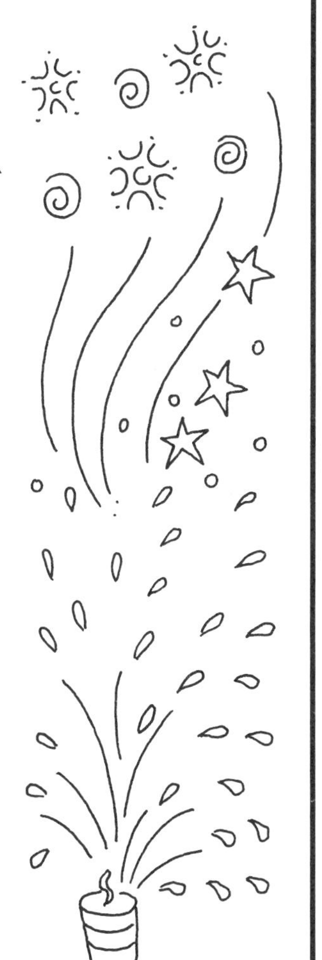

HUNG HEY FAT CHOY

Name ____________

Lucky bag

Lucky bags containing money are given to children at Chinese New Year.
✤ Make a lucky bag using red paper. Use yellow or gold in the decoration.
Two suggestions for decorations are a Chinese dragon or a cut-paper design.

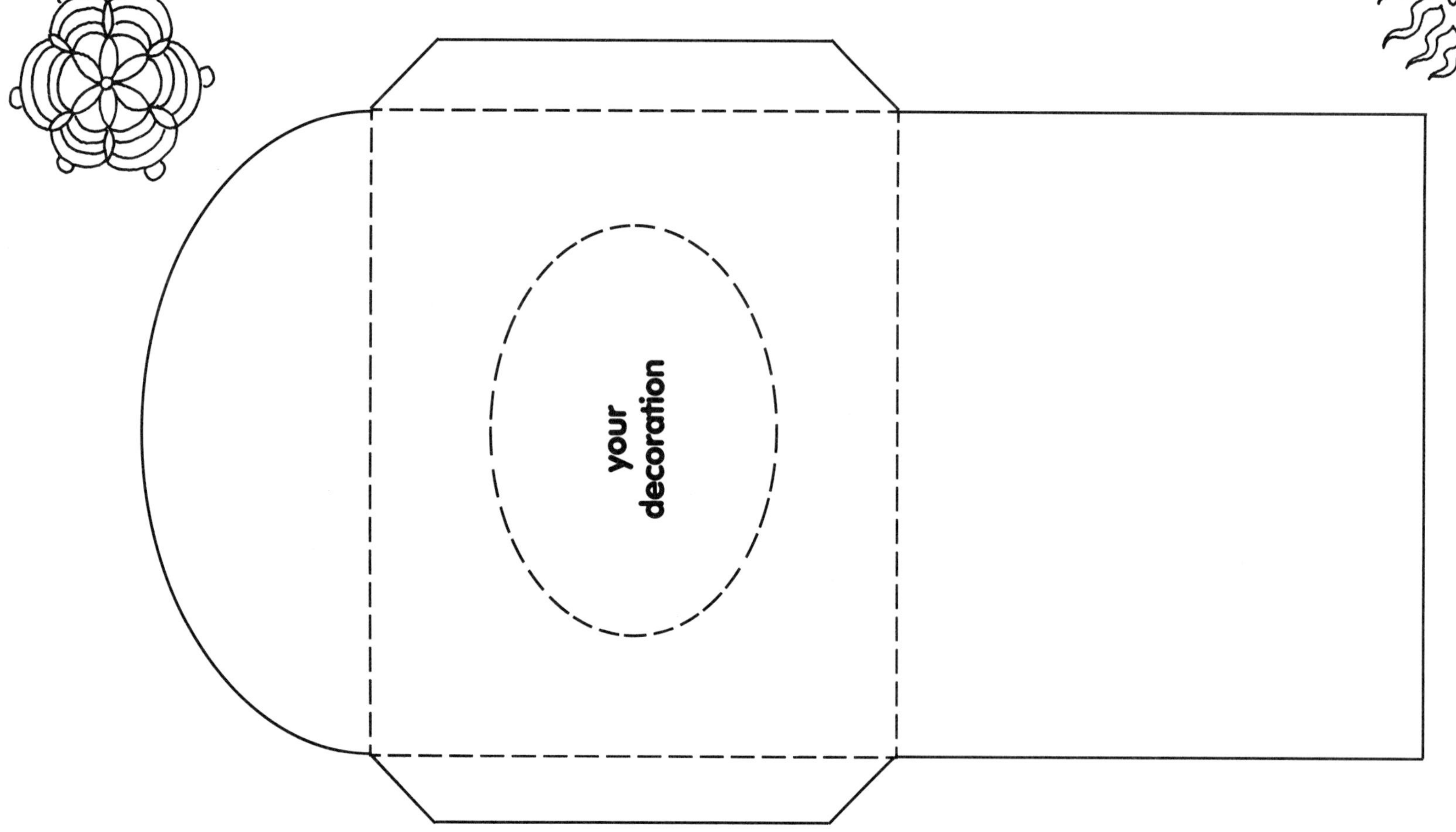

Pancake recipe

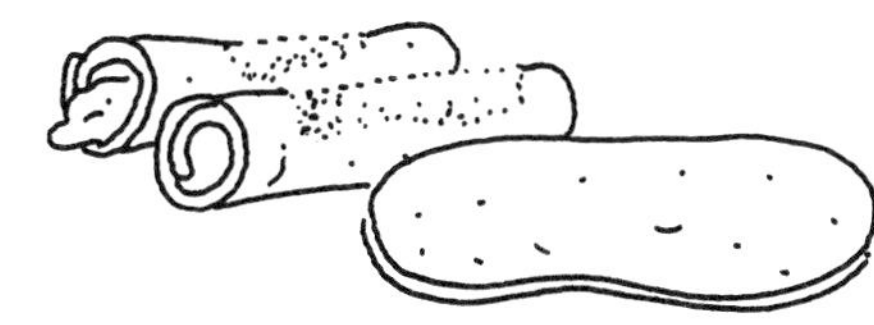

Pancakes are a delicious way to use up food before Lent.

What you need

- 100g flour
- 1 egg
- 300mls milk
- salt
- oil for frying
- sugar
- 1 lemon (halved)
- sieve
- frying pan
- mixing bowl
- wooden spoon

What to do

- Sieve the flour and salt together.
- Add the egg and some of the milk. Mix to a stiff batter.
- Beat well.
- Add the rest of the milk to make a thin batter.
- Heat some oil in the frying pan.

YOU WILL NEED AN ADULT TO HELP YOU WITH THIS

- Pour in enough batter to cover the bottom of the pan.
- Cook until golden brown on the underside.
- Toss and cook the second side.
- Tip the pancake on to a plate.
- Sprinkle with sugar and squeeze on some lemon juice.
- Roll up the pancake.
- ENJOY THE PANCAKES WITH YOUR FRIENDS!

✤ Organise a pancake race with your friends.

Name ______________

Carnival in Europe

Carnival was taken to the Caribbean from Europe.

✤ Find out all you can about carnival in France or Germany.

✤ Draw a picture that shows how it is celebrated.

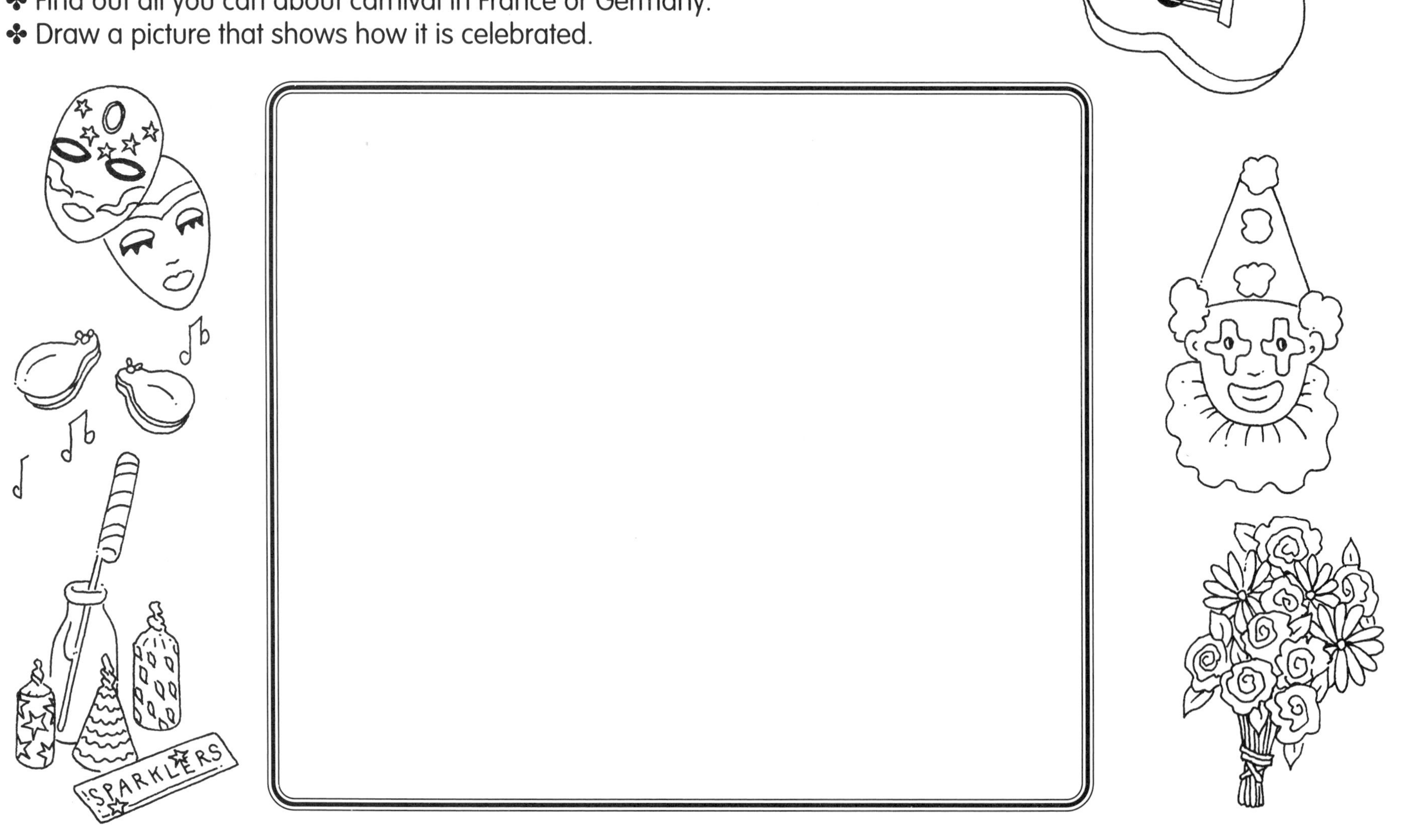

Lent survey

As a way of remembering when Christ was in the wilderness many Christians give up some luxuries during Lent.

✤ Conduct a survey to find out what your friends would choose to give up.

Lent survey

Name	I will give up...

✤ Record your data in a graph.

Name ____________________

St David's Day assembly

The story of Holi

A long time ago, in India, there was a king called Hiranyakashup who had a son called Prahlad.

The king wanted everyone to think of him as God and to worship him. As Prahlad grew up he realised that this was not true and refused to worship his father.

Hiranyakashup was very angry and punished his son. However, Prahlad still refused to worship him and so the king decided that his son must die. The king tried many different ways to kill Prahlad. He was put in a pit full of snakes, he was beaten by soldiers and he was trampled by elephants, but each time Prahlad prayed to Vishnu and he was saved.

The king's sister, Holika, agreed to help the king. She was thought to have magical powers which made her fireproof. Holika took Prahlad to the top of a bonfire and the bonfire was lit. Holika expected Prahlad to die. Instead, it was Holika who died and again Prahlad was saved.

Every year, at the time of Holi, Hindus light bonfires to remind them of this time when good triumphed over evil.

Name ____________________

Celebrating Holi

Holi is celebrated by people throwing coloured powder or water at each other.

✤ What can you see in this picture?

Name ___________________

Holi in the Caribbean

In the Caribbean Hindus celebrate Holi by decorating the walls and floors of their homes and visiting friends. They give each other gifts and garlands and rub 'abrack' (red powder) or 'abeer' (brightly coloured water) on each other. There are also fairs, shows and dancing.

✤ Use the illustrations below to design your own cards and decorations.

leaf designs

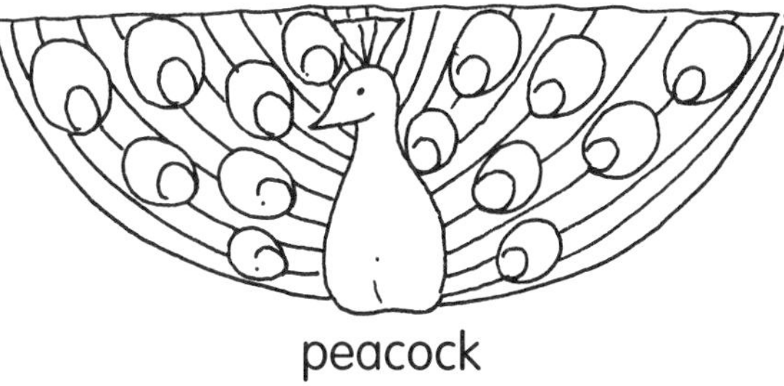

peacock designs

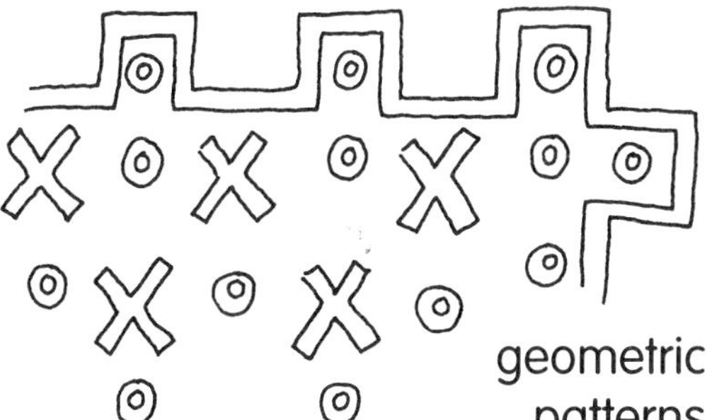

geometric patterns

designs based on the mango

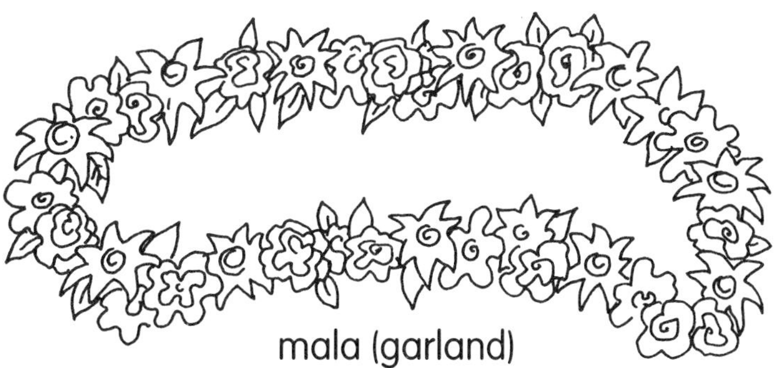

mala (garland)
In the Caribbean this would be made of hibiscus, oleanders and frangipani flowers

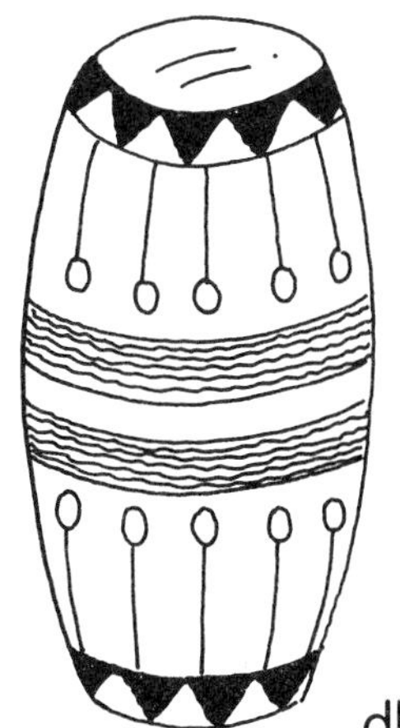

dholak

Name ______________________

The Holi story

✤ Retell the story of Holi as a cartoon.

✤ Use these cartoons to make a 'story scroll'

Name ______________________

You are invited to take part in our

HOLLA MAHALLA Festival

Come and enjoy the fun!

Name ______________

The story of Esther

✤ Fill in the gaps in this story with the words written around the side.

killed

sons

gallows

Jews

king

This story took place in Ancient Persia (Iran). At this time Ahasuerus was king and the __________ was a man called Haman. Haman was angry because a __________ man called Mordecai, refused to bow down to him. Haman tricked the king into agreeing that all the Jews should be __________ .

However, the __________ was Jewish herself. Her name was __________ and she was Mordecai's niece. She exposed Haman's __________ to the king and explained that it would mean that she too would have to die. The __________ was furious and ordered that __________ and his __________ should be killed on the __________ which had been prepared for the __________ __________ then became Prime Minister in his place.

plan

Esther

queen

Haman

Mordecai

Jewish

Prime Minister

Haman's hat biscuits

What you need

- 50g margarine
- 50g sugar
- 75g plain flour
- 25g ground almonds or finely chopped nuts
- ½ teaspoon cinnamon
- mixing bowl
- baking tray
- round cutter
- rolling pin
- spoons
- cooling rack

What to do

- Heat the oven to 180°C or gas mark 4.
- Lightly flour the baking tray.
- Beat together the margarine and sugar, and gradually add the flour. Knead well.
- Lightly roll the mixture and use the round cutter to cut out circles.
- Pinch the edges of the dough to make the shape of a three-cornered hat.
- Place the biscuits on the baking tray (well spaced out) and sprinkle cinnamon on to the centre of each one.
- Bake for 15 to 20 minutes.
- Cool on a wire rack.

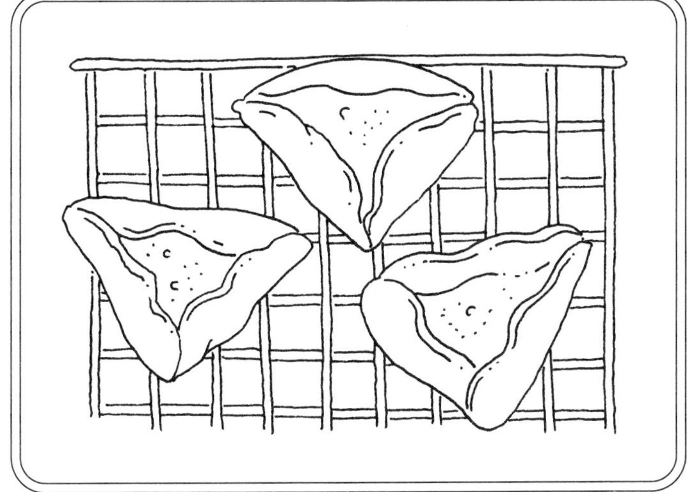

Name ____________________

Make a gregger

When the Purim story is told in the synagogue the gregger is used to drown out the sound of Haman's name.

What you need
- 2 yoghurt pots
- dried beans or peas
- glue or adhesive tape
- materials to decorate

What to do
- Put the peas or beans into the pots – not too many or they won't rattle.
- Stick the two pots together – they need to be well-fixed so that they are secure when rattled.
- Decorate the pots.

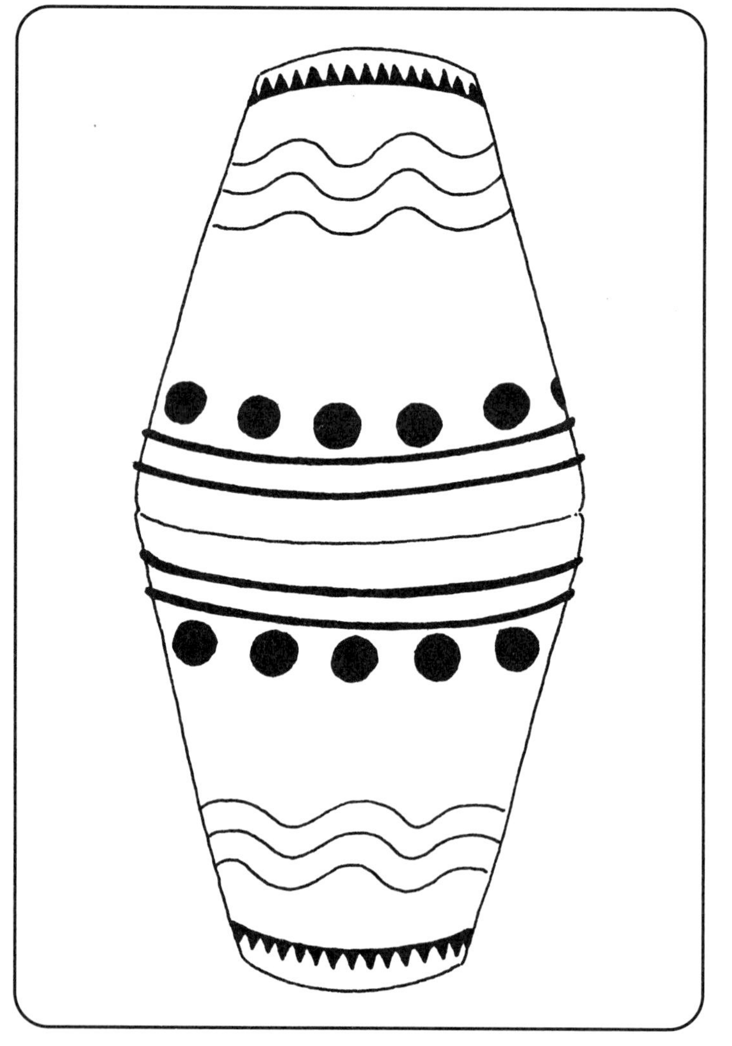

Mask of Haman

❖ Use this outline to make a mask of Haman.

Name ____________________

Japanese/Hina Matsuri (Doll Festival or Girls' Day)

Dolls' Festival

Name ____________________

Setting free the fish and birds

During the Sangkran festival, caged birds and fish are set free.

✤ Colour in these fish and birds and make a display or mobile.

Name ____________________

Visiting the Mother Church

✤ Use the plan on the opposite page to help you with the following.

• This church has three doors:
(a) in the south wall of the porch;
(b) in the north wall, opposite (a) and between the pews and a tomb;
(c) in the west wall of the tower.
Draw them on the plan.
• What are the coordinates for the lectern and the altar cloth box?
• Write down the directions for getting from:
(a) the font to the children's corner;
(b) the porch to the organ.

✤ Make up similar questions and ask a friend to answer them.

✤ Visit your local church and see if you can find similar features there.

✤ Make a plan of your local church. When you return to school you can devise some questions about this church.

Name ____________________

Visiting the Mother Church – plan

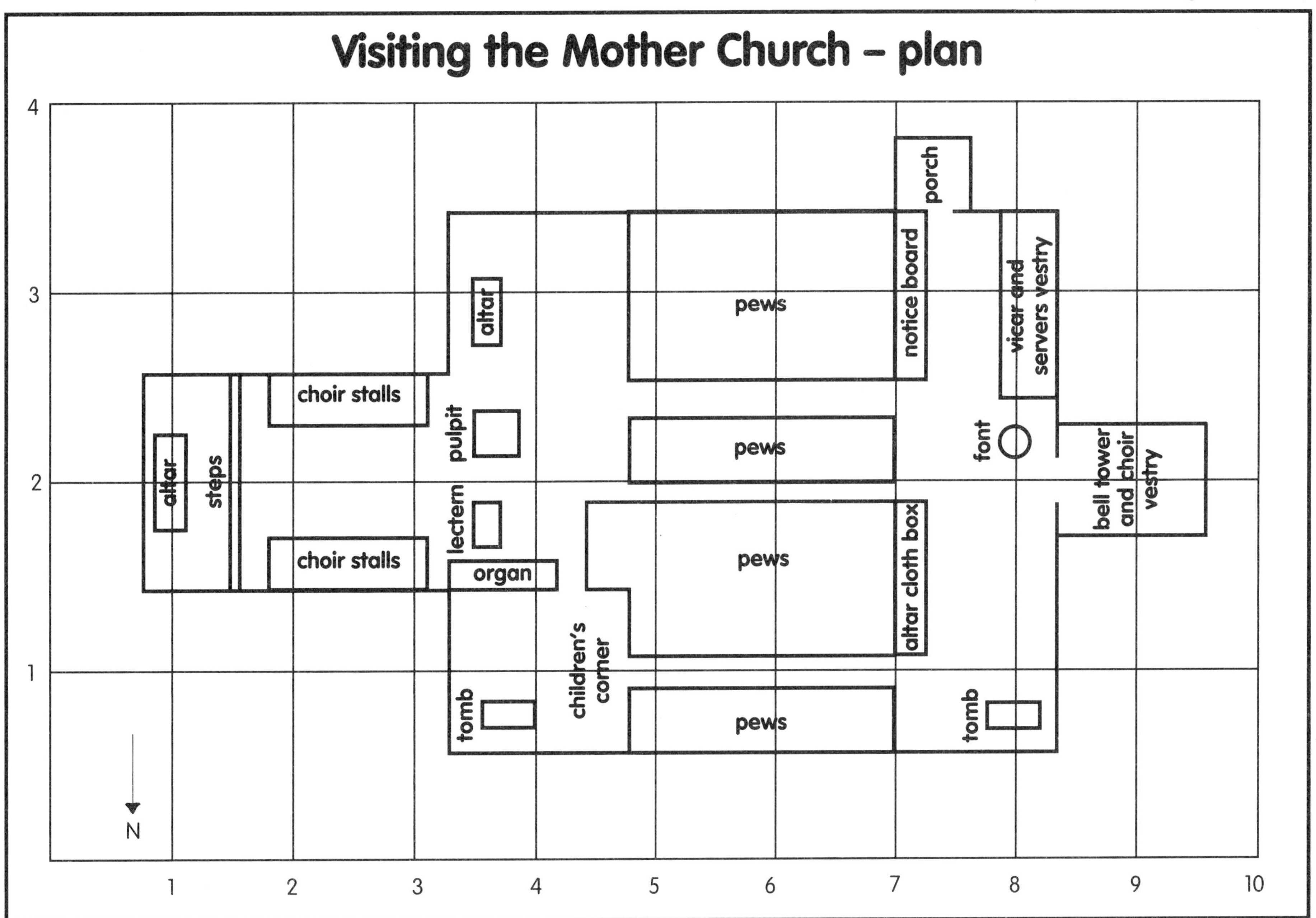

Name ________________

St Patrick's Day assembly

Research

The exact date for the start of Ramadan depends on the moon.

✤ Use a diary or newspaper to record the dates of the new and full moons.

✤ Use this information and your own observations to decide:

• how many days there are between new moons;

• how far apart the full moons appear.

✤ Draw diagrams to explain why this happens. You can use library books to help you.

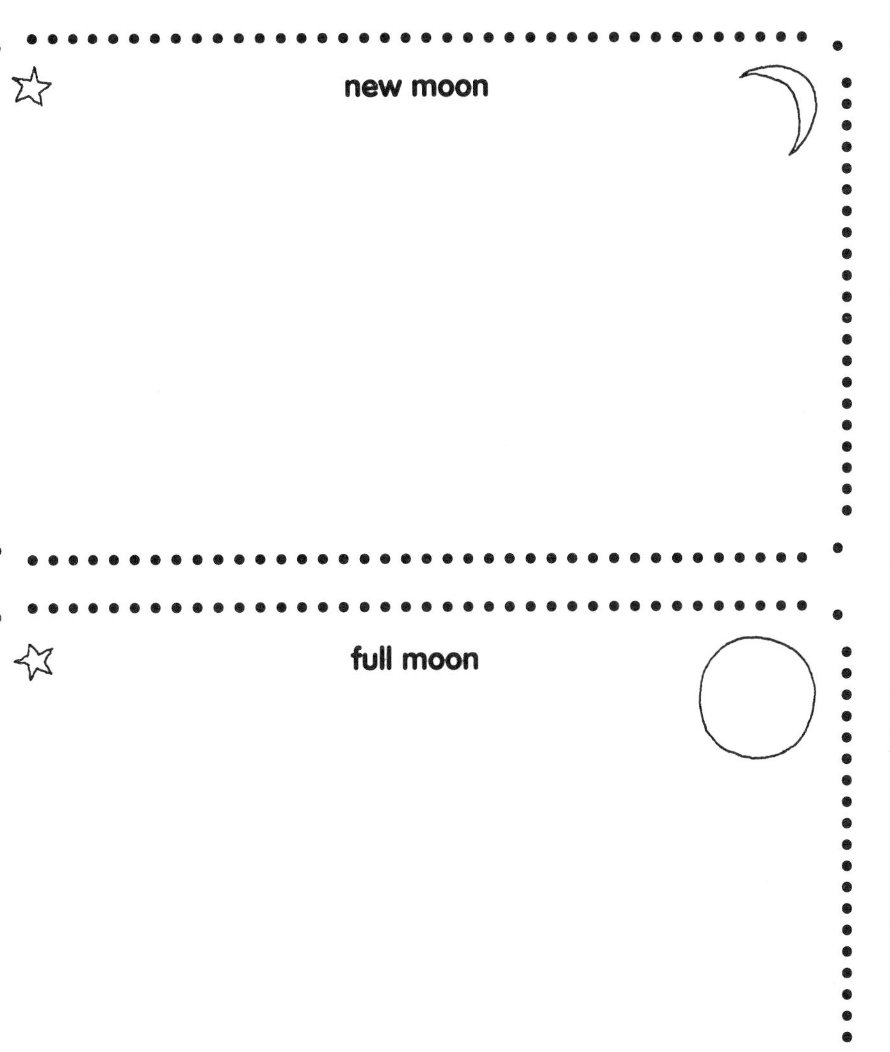

Name ____________

Class trip

Dear Parent

Class __________ has been finding out about ____________ and as a part of this topic they are going on a class trip to the __________ Mandir. They will leave at __________ and return at approx. _________ on _________.

If you would like to take advantage of this opportunity it might be possible for you to accompany us. Places are limited but we would like as many parents as possible to join us.

We have permission for children to take photographs. Please contact me before letting your child bring her/his camera.

Yours sincerely

✂ -

I give/do not give permission for _________ to go on the class visit to __________ on ______________.
I would/would not like to join the class for this visit.

Signed ______________________________
(parent/ guardian)
Date ______________________________

Name ____________

Lotus decoration

Flowers are a reminder that the Buddha is said to have been born in a garden.

✤ Use the lotus shape to make a decoration or greetings card.

Name ______________________

The procession

Traditionally, churches are decorated with palms or greenery for Palm Sunday. Often congregations meet in one church where palms are blessed and then they walk in procession to a neighbouring church for communion.

✤ Draw a picture of the procession with the participants carrying crosses.

The Passover story

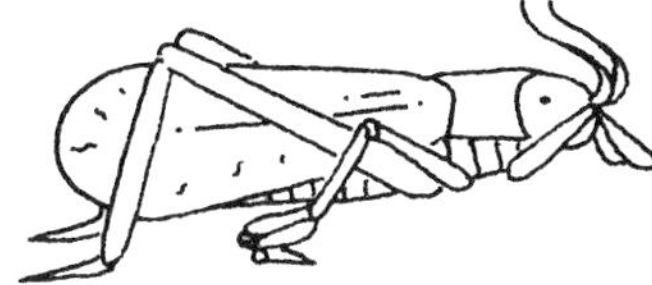

In Egypt, Jewish people were treated as slaves. Moses went to Pharaoh to ask him to release the slaves but this request was refused. To punish the Egyptians, God sent the 'Plagues' – blood, frogs, lice, wild beasts, blight, boils, hail, locusts, and darkness. Each plague was more terrible than the last.

Pharaoh still wouldn't release the Jews and so God sent a terrible punishment – all the Egyptian first-born sons were to die. Moses told the Jewish families to kill a lamb and daub its blood on their front doors so that the 'Angel of Death' would know that it was a Jewish home and pass over without killing their sons.

After this punishment, Pharaoh begged Moses to take his people and leave Egypt. He didn't think that the Egyptians could stand any more punishment. The Jews prepared quickly and began their long search for the 'Promised Land'.

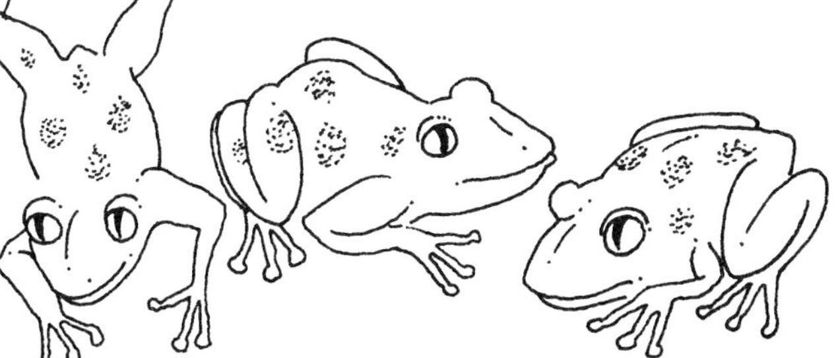

Name ____________________

Pesach (Passover) quiz

1 What do Jewish people celebrate at Pesach (Passover)? ____________________

2 What were the ten plagues? ____________________

3 Who lead the Israelites out of Israel? ____________________

4 What is a 'Seder plate'? ____________________

5 What are the symbolic items on the Seder plate? ____________________

6 Who asks the questions during the meal? ____________________

7 How many questions are asked? ____________________

8 What is the Haggadah? ____________________

9 Why do Jewish people traditionally give their homes a thorough clean before Pesach? ____________________

10 During the week of the festival, what is eaten instead of bread? ____________________

Charoset recipe

What you need
- 2 apples
- ½ cup chopped walnuts
- 1 teaspoon cinnamon
- 2 tablespoons apple juice
- a few chopped dates and raisins
- a measuring spoon and cup
- bowls
- a grater

What to do
- Grate the apples.
- Add the walnuts, fruit and cinnamon. Mix well.
- Add the apple juice and mix.

Name ____________________

Symbols of Pesach (Passover)

✤ Match each symbol with its meaning. The first one is done for you.

Bitter herbs (horseradish) ————	A reminder of the hard times faced by the Israelites in Egypt.
Charoset	A reminder of the taste of the Israelites' tears.
Salt water	Symbol of joy and freedom.
Cup of wine	To remember the speed at which the Israelites left Egypt – they didn't have time to let their bread rise.
Roasted egg	A symbol of relaxation after slavery.
Matzah	Represents the Paschal lamb which would have been sacrificed in gratitude.
Shank bone of lamb	A sign of spring and a reminder of God's provision of food.
Cushions on chairs	A reminder of the cement used to build palaces and cities in Egypt.
Green herbs (parsley)	A symbol of new life and a reminder of the festival offerings in the last temple.

Baisakhi – the play

✤ Make up a play that tells the story.

REMEMBER THAT IT IS OFFENSIVE TO MOST SIKHS IF ANY GURU IS PORTRAYED.

✤ Can you find a way to act the story without showing the leading character?

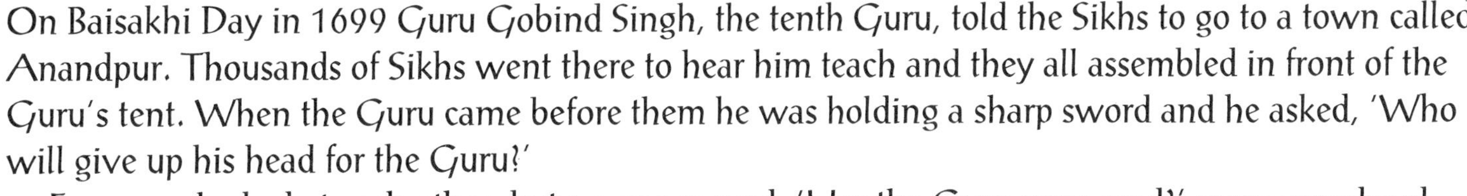

On Baisakhi Day in 1699 Guru Gobind Singh, the tenth Guru, told the Sikhs to go to a town called Anandpur. Thousands of Sikhs went there to hear him teach and they all assembled in front of the Guru's tent. When the Guru came before them he was holding a sharp sword and he asked, 'Who will give up his head for the Guru?'

Everyone looked at each other, but no one moved. 'Has the Guru gone mad?' some wondered. At last one man stepped forward. The Guru took him into his tent and the crowd heard the swish of his sword. The Guru came out of his tent alone, and his sword was dripping with blood.

Once again he asked, 'Who will give up his head for the Guru?' After much shuffling of feet another man stepped forward and again he was taken into the tent and again the sound of a sword was heard.

The Guru repeated his question three more times and after the fifth man had been taken into the tent the Guru came out followed by all five men who were alive and unharmed.

These men became known as the Five Beloved Ones (Panj Pyare) because of their bravery and loyalty. The Guru said that they were an example to all Sikhs and showed how they should be willing to die for their faith.

The Guru asked these five men to perform the same ceremony and by the end of the day most of the crowd had been initiated in the same way. These people became known as the Khalsa (the pure or dedicated ones).

From that time onwards, Sikhs took up the custom of sharing the same name as a sign of equality. This is why Sikh men are called Singh, which means 'lion', and all women are called Kaur, which means 'princess'.

Name ______________________

Symbols and uniforms

Sikhs who are baptised into the Khalsa believe in equality for all and peace.
✤ What characteristics do you associate with other symbols or uniforms?

Symbol or uniform	**Characteristic**
Sikh	equality, peace
St John's	gentle, volunteer, knowledge of first aid
Scouts	

Name ____________________

The five Ks

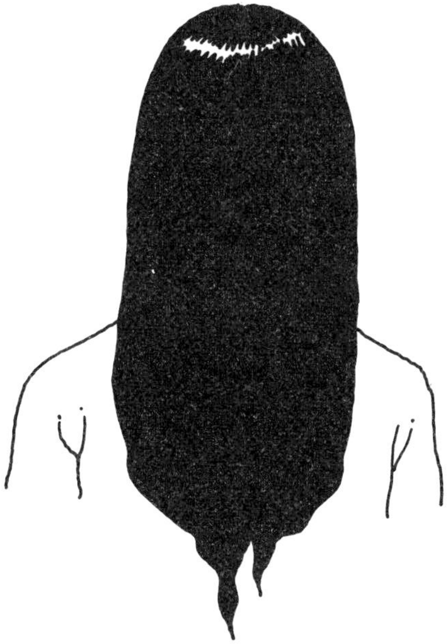

Kesh (uncut hair)

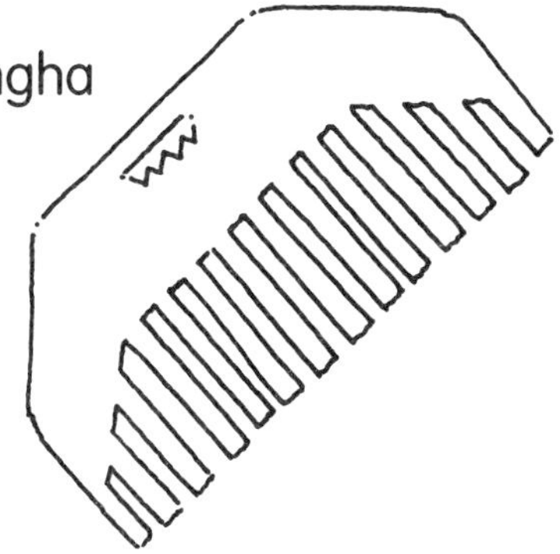

Kangha

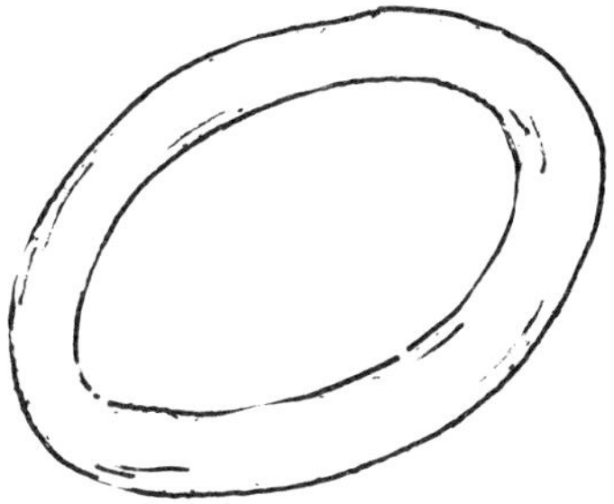

Kara (bracelet)

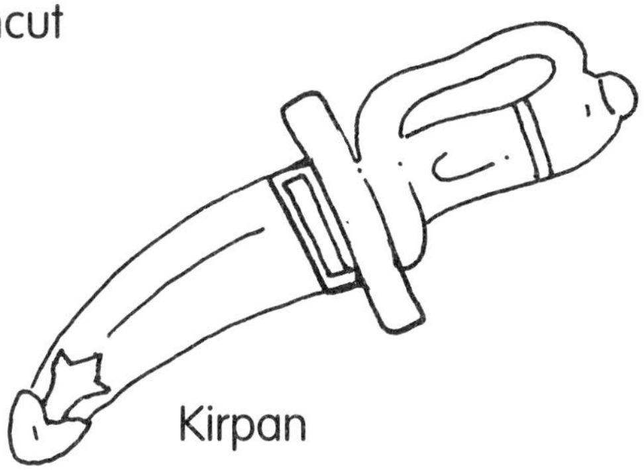

Kirpan

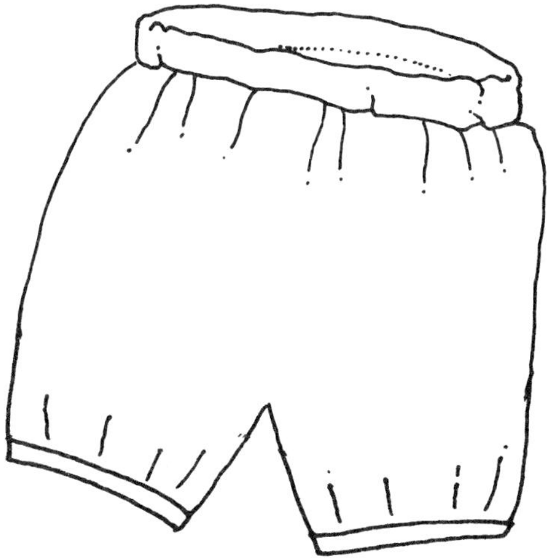

Kachha

Name ____________

Panj kakke

Sikhs are taught that their hair is a gift from God. Therefore, it should not be cut and it must be properly looked after – combed and washed.

ਕੇਸ

Sikhs wear a ring of steel around the wrist of the hand that will use the kirpan. It is both a symbol of equality and a symbol that God is never-ending like a circle.

ਕੜਾ

This might be worn in the hair or carried in a pocket. A boy's hair might be tied in a jura on top of his head.

ਕਿਰਪਾਨ

This is worn around the neck or on a halter over the shoulder. It shows that Sikhs will fight in self-defence. It is only opened in self-defence.

ਕਛ

Cotton shorts are worn as underwear. They used to be part of a soldier's clothes and were designed to allow them to move easily. It is a symbol of being ready to act whenever necessary.

Name ____________________

The Easter story

✤ Cut out these cards and arrange them in the correct order to tell the Easter story.

Jesus prepared to ride into Jerusalem for the Passover Festival. He rode on a donkey. The people of Jerusalem welcomed Jesus as a king.	Jesus visited the temple. He was so angry when He saw how it was being treated that He turned over the tables. This made the priests very angry.	Two days before Passover Judas visited the chief priests and arranged to betray Jesus.
Jesus and the disciples met for the Passover meal. He warned them of what was to happen. This was to become known as 'The Last Supper'. After the meal Jesus was betrayed and arrested.	Jesus was questioned by the High Priests. They found Him guilty but they needed the Roman Emperor's permission to kill Him. Judas was sorry for what he had done.	Jesus was questioned by Pontius Pilate who wanted to set Him free. It was the custom that one person should be set free during Passover. The crowd wanted it to be Barabbas (a murderer). They wanted to crucify Jesus .
Jesus was tortured and forced to carry the cross for His crucifixion at Golgotha. This was on 'Good Friday'.	Joseph of Arimathaea was allowed to take His body and place it in a guarded tomb.	Jesus appeared to his followers. He asked them to spread the news about His life and death.

Name ____________

Press coverage

✣ Imagine that you are a journalist and a friend of Jesus Christ. Write the story of what happened to Him. Don't forget the headline and caption.

JERUSALEM GAZETTE

✣ Write the story from the point of view of the High Priest.

Decorated eggs

What to do

- Hard boil a white-shelled egg in natural dye – use onion skins for yellow; use beetroot for red; use spinach leaves for green; or a few drops of food dye.
- Decorate the eggs with felt-tips or paint.

In Eastern Europe eggs are decorated with a method using wax.

✤ Find out how to do this.

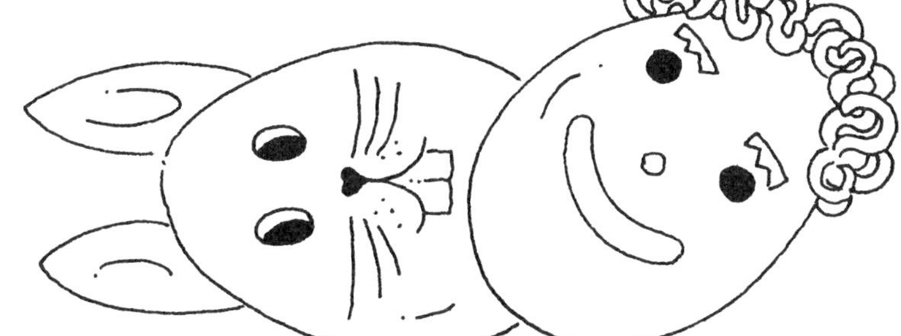

Hard-boiled eggs can be decorated to look like human and animal faces.

✤ Use junk materials to create a character.

Name ____________

Easter card

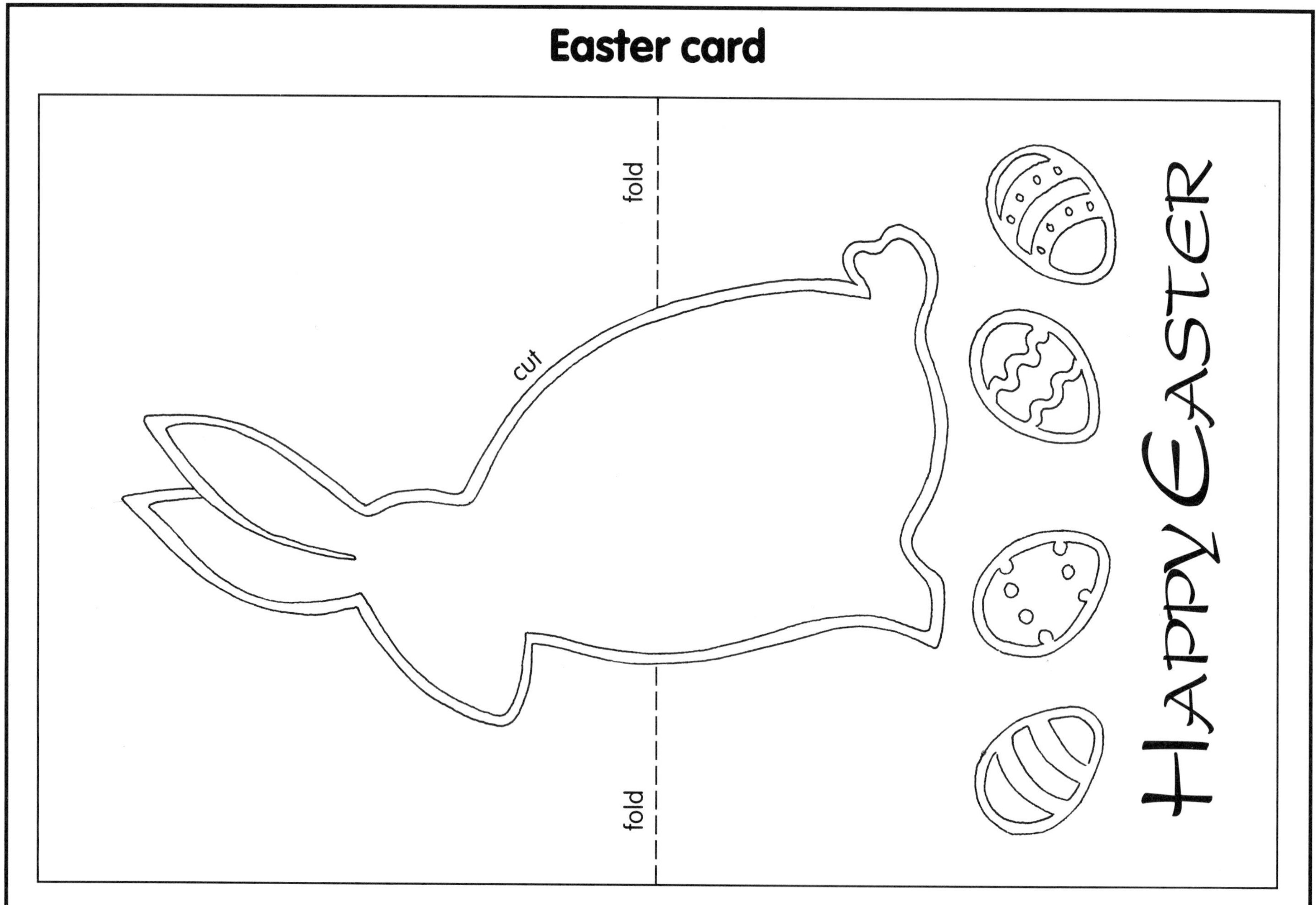

Name ____________________

One country

During the Ridvan celebrations Baha'i children enjoy parties.

✤ Design a party hat or decoration that will illustrate the saying of Baha'u'llah.

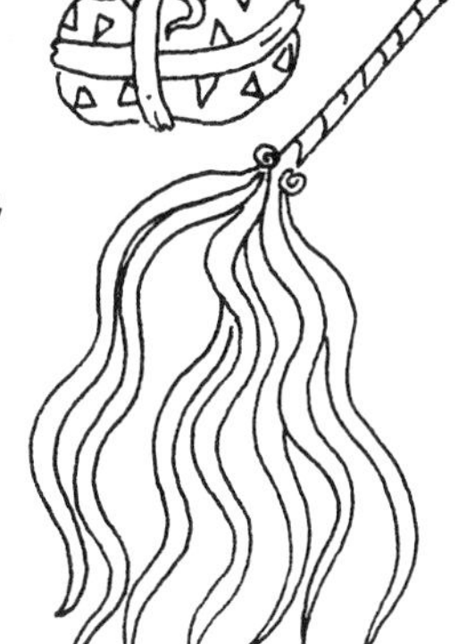

'The earth is one country and mankind its citizens'

Baha' u' llah.

Name ________________

St George's Day assembly

Festival of Labour

Since the nineteenth century the first day of May has been celebrated as a Festival of Labour Day. On this day workers take part in processions, often led by works bands, and with each trade union carrying a banner. These banners had mottoes on them such as 'Justice for All'.

✤ Work in groups to find out about the conditions of workers in the nineteenth century, decide on a trade and a motto for your banner.

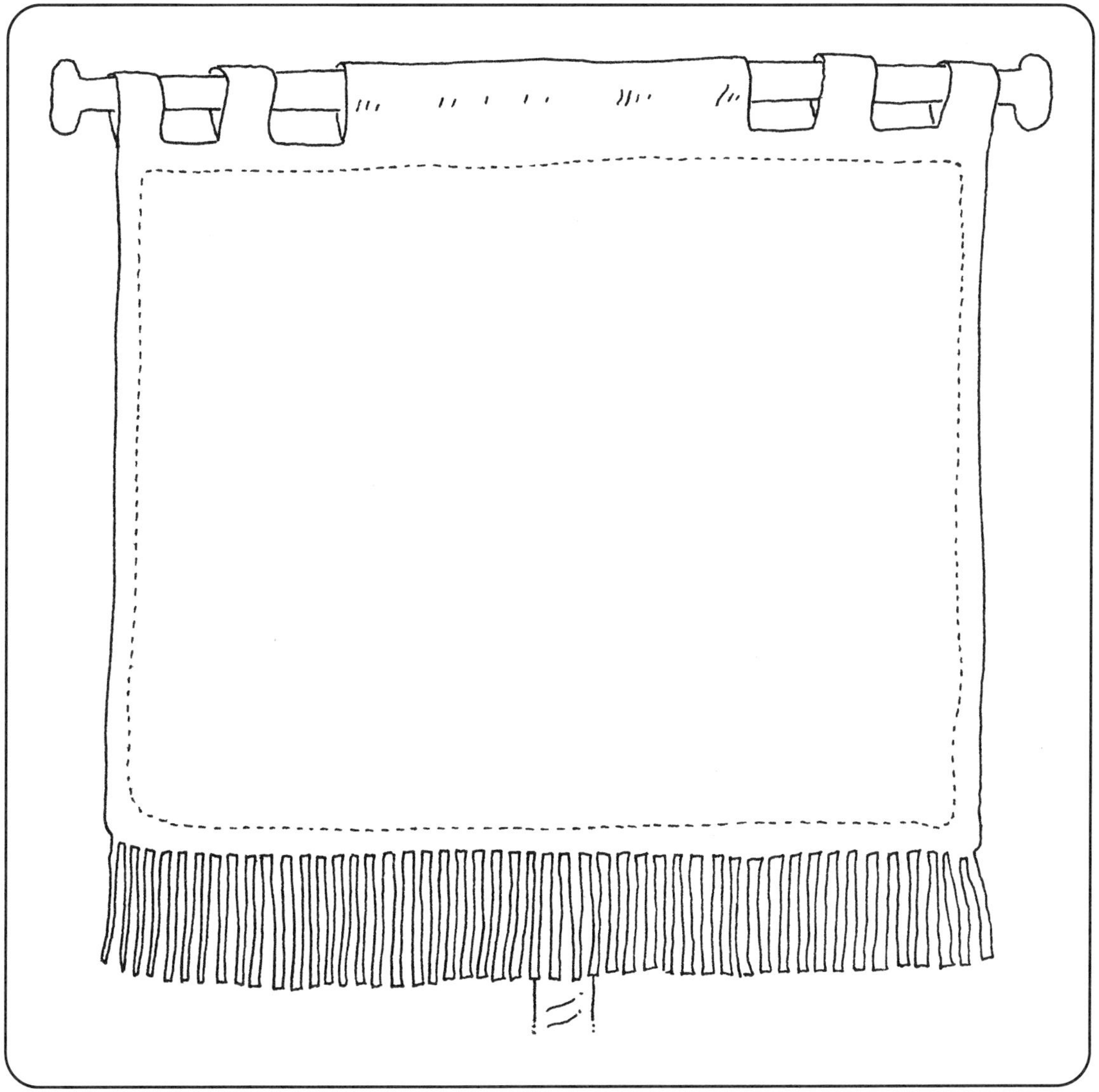

Name ______________________

The 'Enlightened One'

The Buddha was known as The Enlightened One. He brought 'light' to others.

✤ How can you be like a light and make other people happy?

✤ Fill your flame with ideas for what you can do. Then you can colour the flames, cut it out and mount it.

Orange lanterns

During this important Buddhist festival, homes and religious buildings are decorated with lanterns and garlands. Here is a decoration to make that could be used for this festival.

What you need

- an orange
- a sharp knife
- a teaspoon
- a night-light
- matches or lighter

You will also need some adult help.

1 Cut an orange in half.

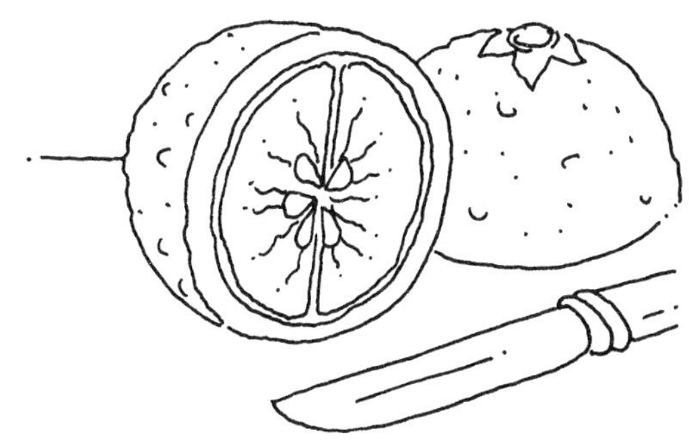

2 Remove the flesh from the orange.

3 Cut a circle, about 3cm in diameter, from the top of the orange.

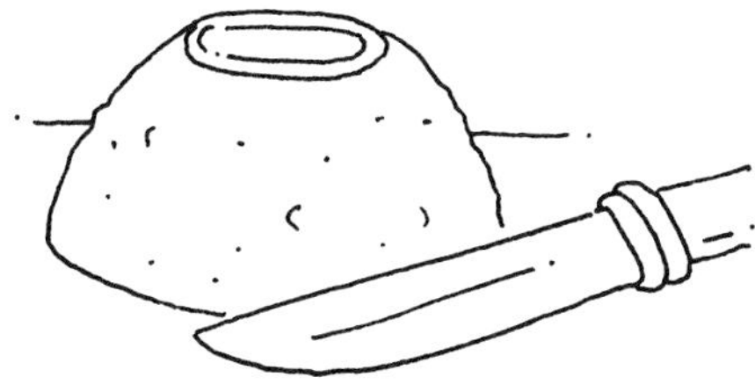

4 Place the night-light in the bottom.

5 Light the night-light and place the top of the orange on top of the base.

Name ____________________

Garlands

During this important Buddhist festival, homes and religious buildings are decorated with lanterns and garlands.

✤ Make some garlands.

What you need
- coloured tissue paper
- scissors
- string

1 Cut out circles of tissue paper. Make cuts all around the edge.

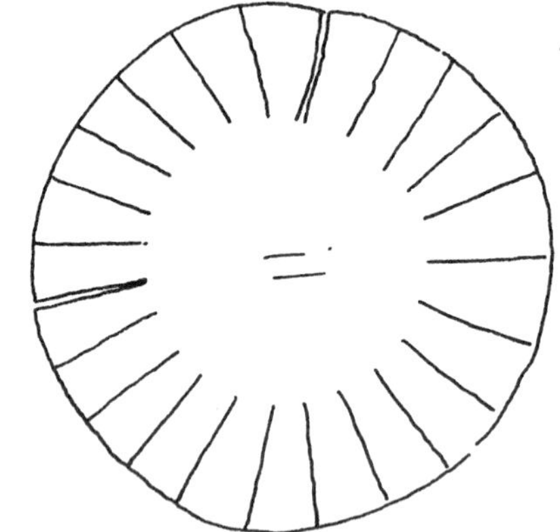

2 'Scrunch' the middle of the circle.

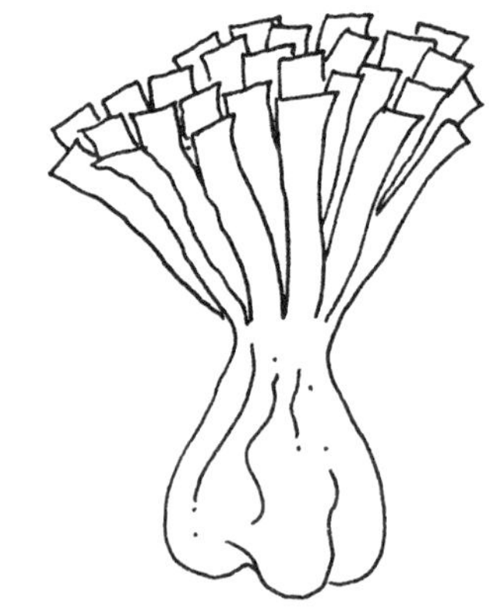

3 Thread the tissue on to string.

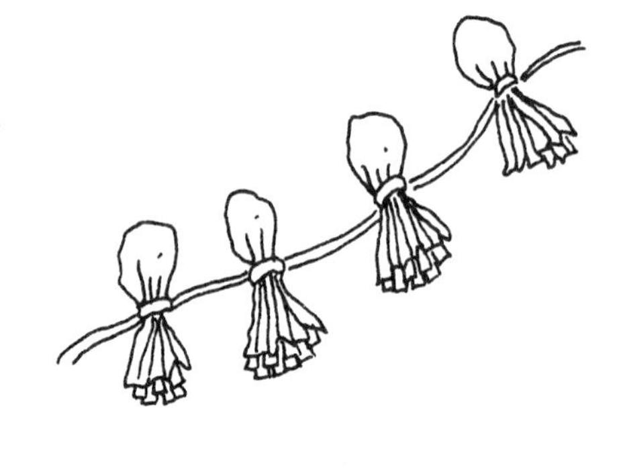

4 Open-out the tissue paper. Form into a garland.

Carp streamers

In Japan, during the festival called Boys' Day carp streamers are made from colourful paper and fixed to trees as decorations.

✤ Make a carp streamer and decorate the classroom.

1 Take a sheet of paper and make it into a roll

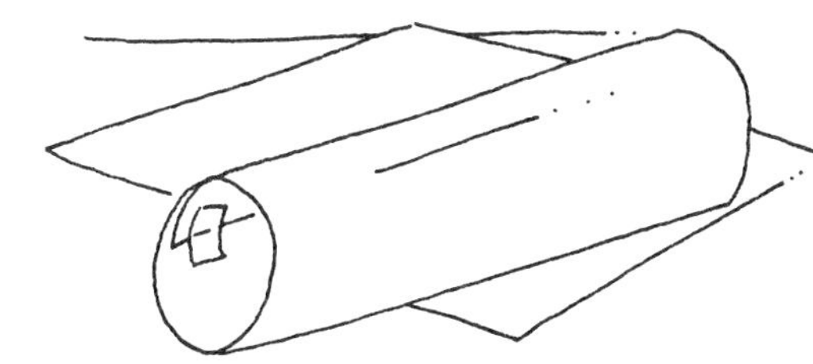

2 Cut out the tail shape.

3 Attach string.

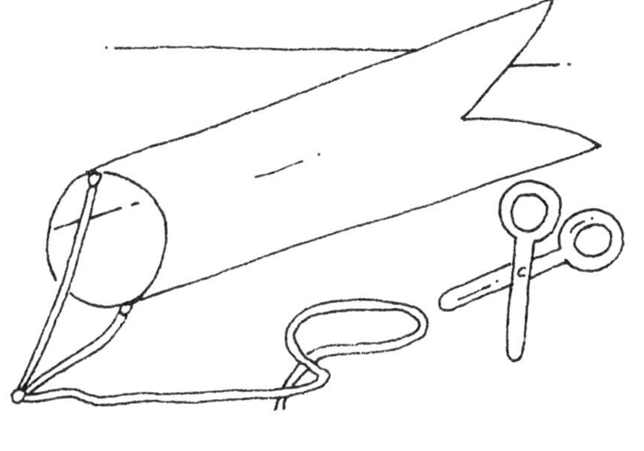

4 Decorate with tissue paper.

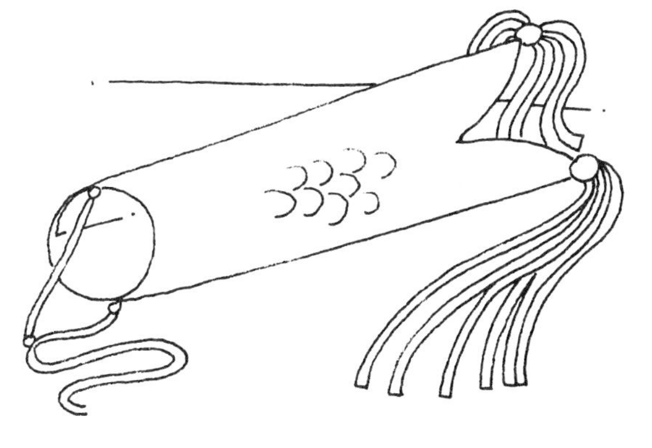

Name ______________

Pin-wheel testing

What you need
- paper; a pencil with eraser; a dress making pin; scissors

What to do
- Use the template opposite to cut out a piece of paper as shown.
- Cut on the dotted lines.
- Fold the corners (ABCD) to meet and slightly overlap in the centre.
- Push a pin through all the corners and E.
- Insert the pin in the eraser of the pencil.

Testing
In testing the pin-wheel the following variations may be tried:
- type of material
- size of material
- length of pin
- length of cuts
- order of folding
- strength of wind

✤ Can you think of any other variations?

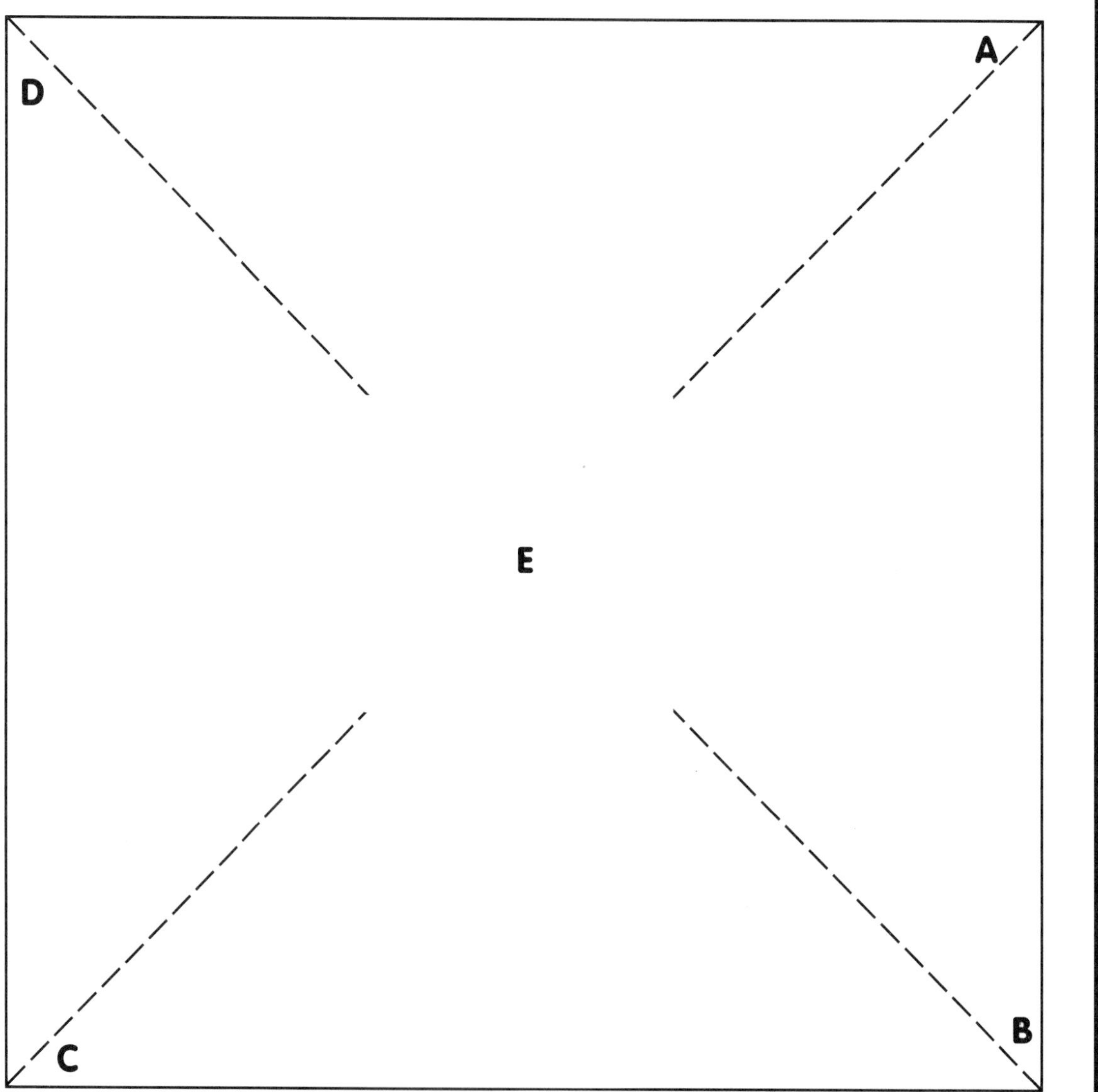

Name ____________________

Allah

✤ Colour the word in shades of green.

Name ____________

Eid-ul-Fitr card

✤ Design and make your own card.

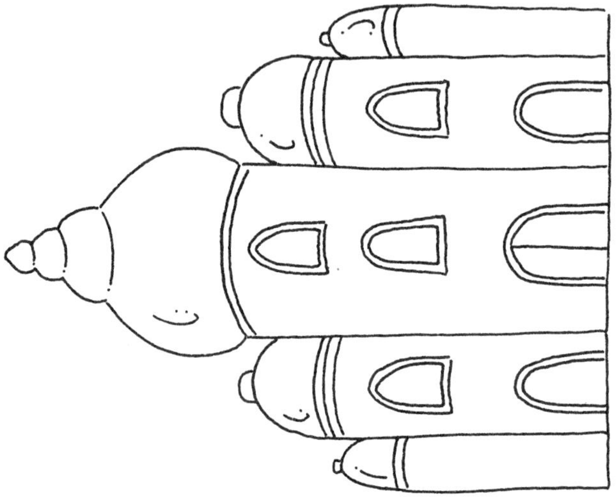

عيد مبارك

Make a mobile

Eid-ul-Fitr is celebrated at the end of Ramadan. It starts when the new moon is sighted.

✤ Use these patterns to make templates. They can be covered with paint, foil, sticky paper, glitter or tissue-paper balls.

Name ________________

Coconut barfi

What you need

- 100g dried milk
- 75g desiccated coconut
- 75g sugar
- 60mls water
- food colouring
- a saucepan
- a mixing bowl
- a baking tray
- a mixing spoon

What to do

- Grease the baking tray.
- Heat the sugar and water together to make a syrup.
- Mix the milk powder and coconut together.
- Put a few drops of colouring into the syrup.
- Add the syrup to the dry mixture. Mix well.
- Spread the mixture on the baking tray.
- Cool the barfi then cut it into squares.

WARNING: HOT SYRUP IS DANGEROUS.
ASK AN ADULT TO HELP.

First fruits

During Shavuot synagogues are decorated with fruit.

✤ Use these templates to help you make some decorations.

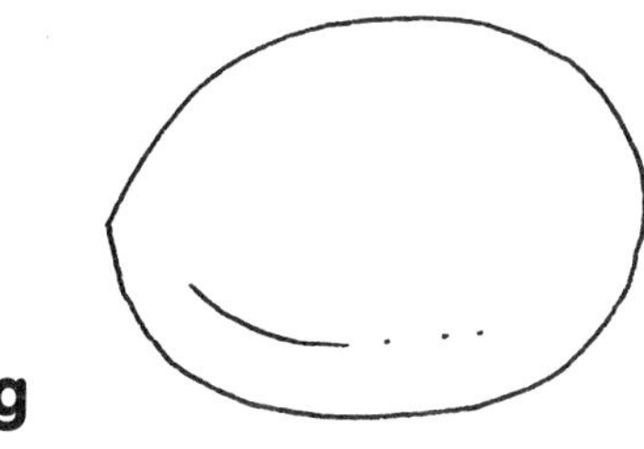

fig

pomegranate

date

grape

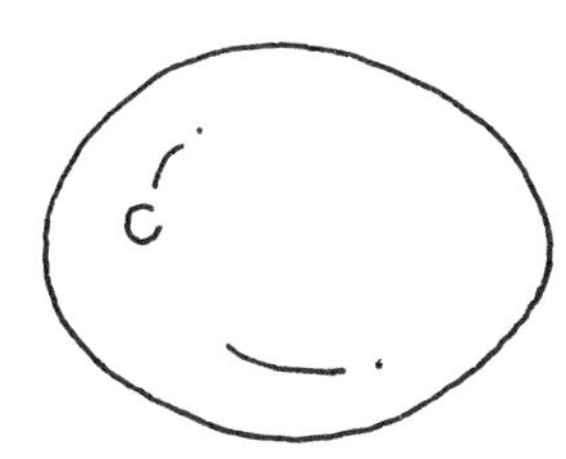

olive

apple

Name ________________

Well dressing

The custom of well dressing takes place in many English villages.

What you need

- a wooden board cut to shape
- clay
- a collection of natural materials such as flowers, moss, shells, seeds, leaves, sticks.

What to do

- Carefully prepare your design.
- Cover the board with smooth clay.
- Draw your design on the clay.
- Fill in the design with the flowers and other materials.
- Tidy up.

✤ Find out what customs there are in your area. Perhaps you could interview local people?

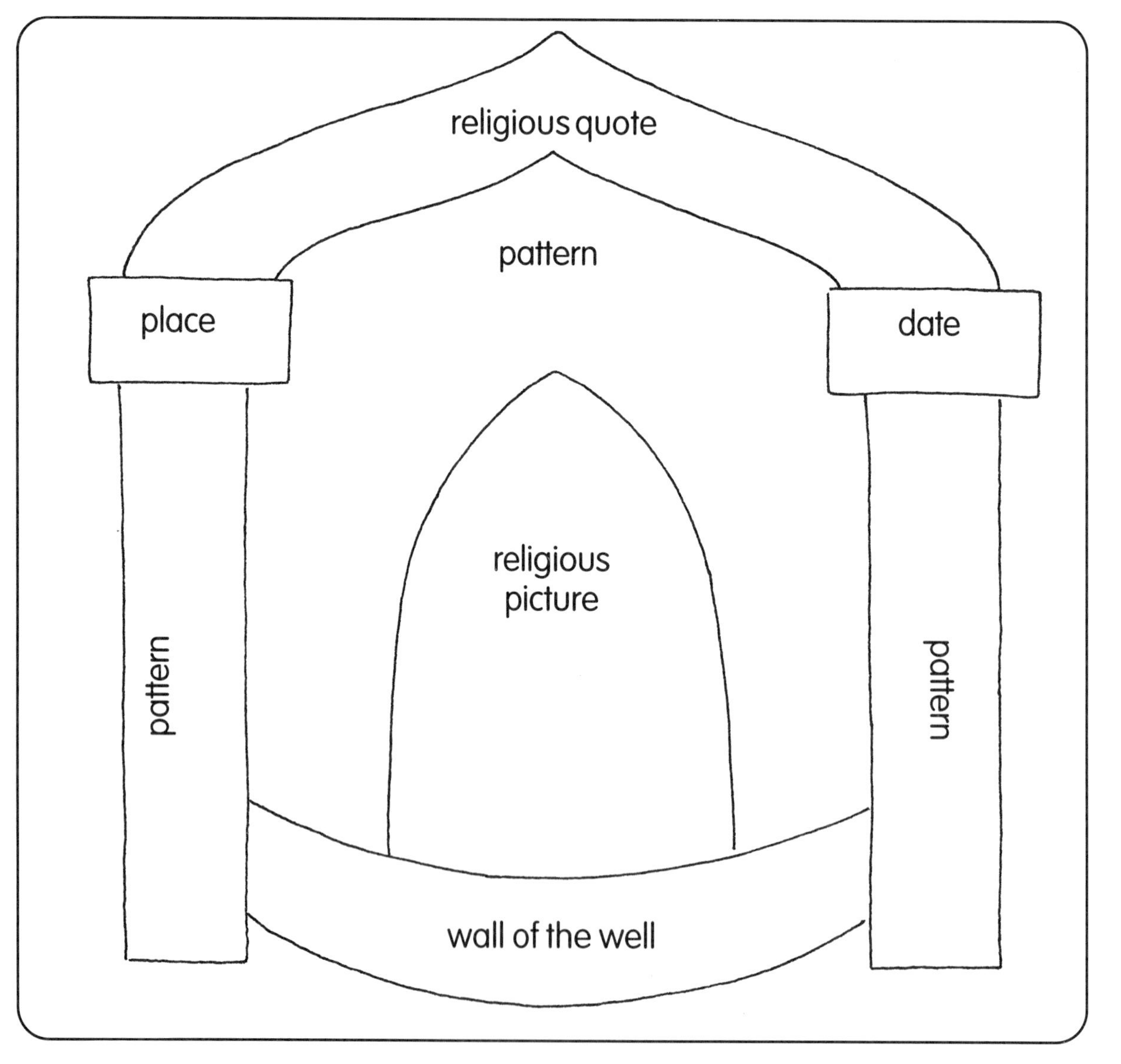

Name ____________________

Whit walk

- Draw a map of an area that is special to you.
- Show the route for a Whit walk and mark the places you feel are important.

Title: ______________________________

N

↑

key

scale

Name ______________

Dragon boats

This festival is a reminder of an event that happened over two thousand years ago. Ch'u Yuan was a statesman who committed suicide in protest against the injustice of the government. To stop the fish (and dragons) from eating his body the people rushed out in boats and threw food to them. Since then people in Hong Kong hold annual dragon boat races. These boats are often 100 feet long and are covered with pictures and lots of colour on them to frighten the fish.

- Draw a picture of a dragon boat below.
- Design and make one.

Name ____________________

Three-in-one

Trinity Sunday is about seeing God in three different forms – the Trinity. Water can also take three forms – liquid, gas and solid.

✤ Conduct experiments to demonstrate that water can take three different forms.

REMEMBER: EXPERIMENTS USING HEAT ARE DANGEROUS. CHECK EVERYTHING WITH YOUR TEACHER.

At room temperature, water is	When heated, water is	When frozen, water is
____________________	____________________	____________________

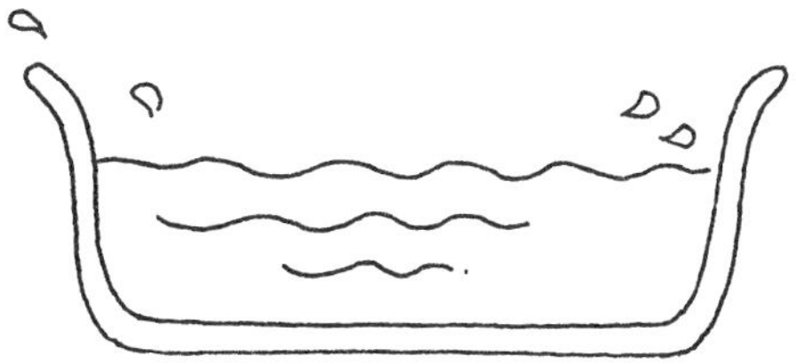

✤ What happens when the gas reaches a cold surface?

✤ What happens when the solid melts?

Name ____________

Word origins

The word 'juggernaut' comes from the name of the Hindu festival of Jagannath.

✤ Find out the language that the following words come from.

anorak ____________	typhoon ____________
shampoo ____________	poodle ____________
bungalow ____________	robot ____________
chocolate ____________	hiccup ____________
ukelele ____________	garage ____________
slogan ____________	piano ____________
yoghurt ____________	carnival ____________
cargo ____________	blonde ____________

Happy Eid – Arabic

Name ______________

Finding the way

✤ Use your atlas to plan the route to Saudi Arabia. Which of the following will you pass?

River Thames
River Nile
River Rhine
River Danube

Jerusalem
London
Paris
Berlin
Rome
Brussels
Amsterdam
Athens

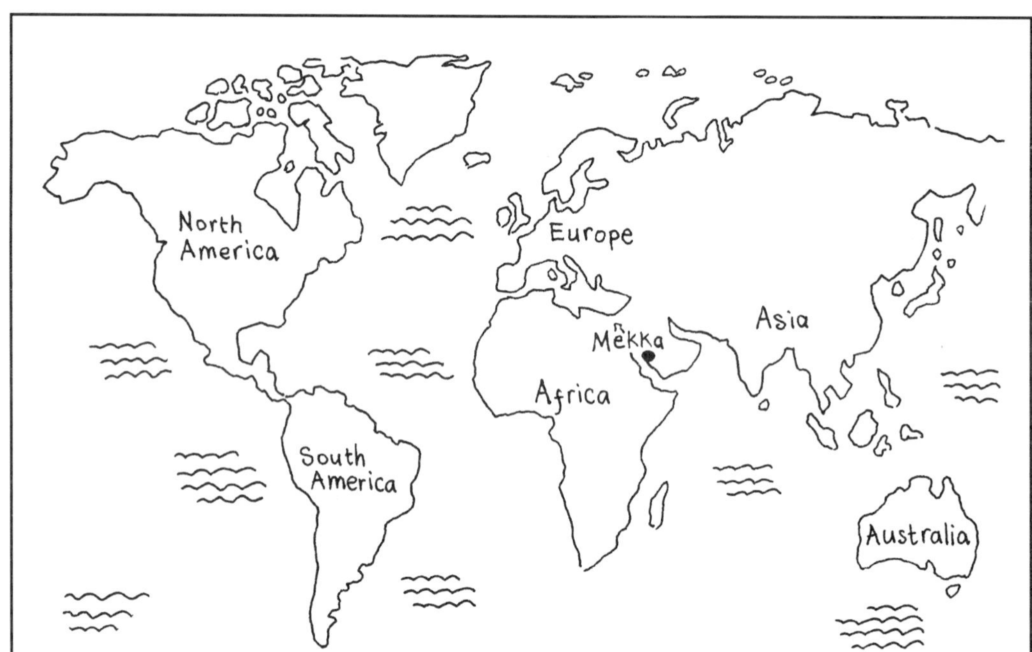

France
Germany
Italy
England
Belgium
Netherlands
Denmark
Greece
Israel
Egypt
Saudi Arabia

Suez Canal

Europe
Africa
Asia

Tropic of Cancer
Alps

The English Channel
The Mediterranean Sea
The North Sea

✤ Work in groups to devise a game using these locations.

Name ____________________

The meaning of Hajj

✤ Find the correct ending for each sentence.

1 Pilgrims wear an Ihram	to show they are all equal.
2 They all wear the same	a stone believed to have been part of the Ka'aba built by Abraham.
3 They walk round the Ka'aba	the well of Zam Zam.
4 The Ka'aba is	as a symbol of giving everything up.
5 Pilgrims drink from	as they walk round the Ka'aba.
6 They recite verses from the Qu'ran	seven times.

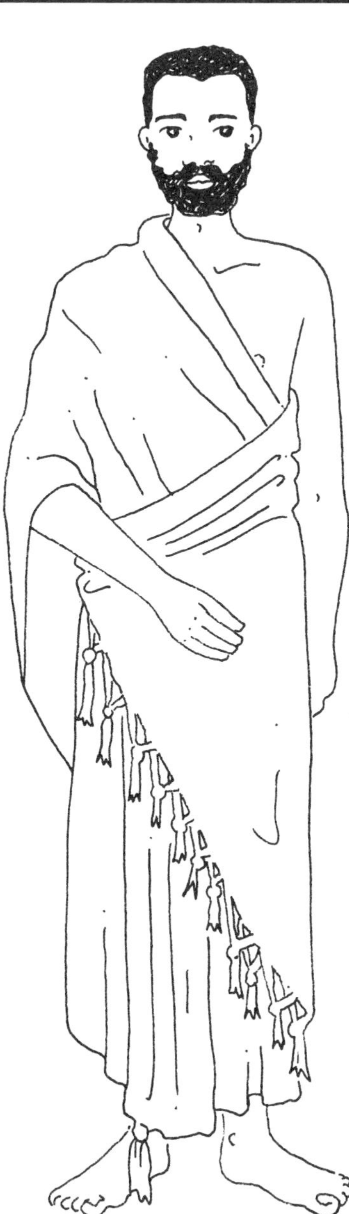

Name ________________

Name ____________________

The wheel of teaching

The wheel is a symbol in Buddhism.

✤ To which religion do these symbols belong?

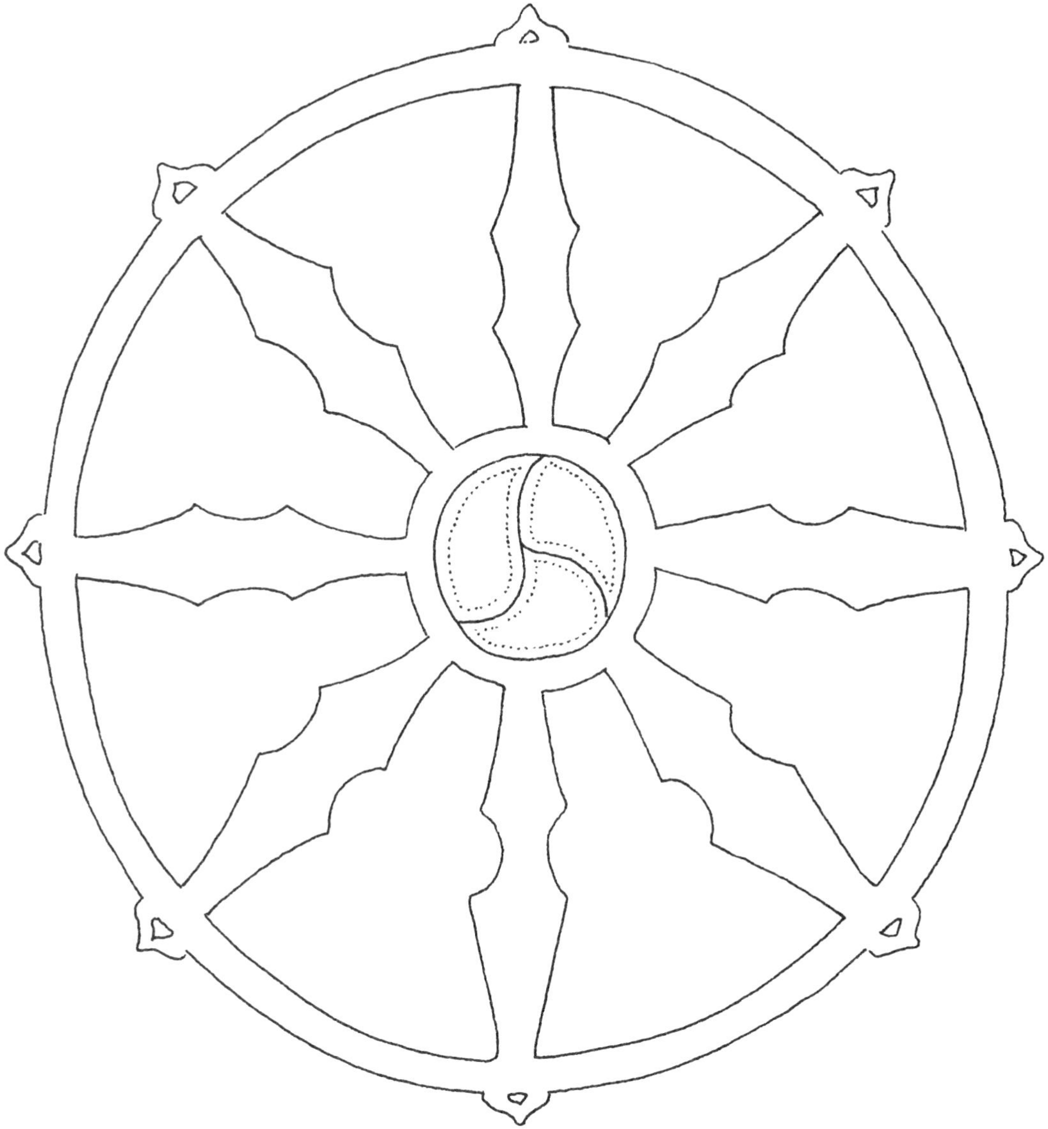

Name ___________________

Exhibition

COME AND SEE OUR

EXHIBITION

TO CELEBRATE THE BIRTHDAY OF

HAILE SELASSIE

AT ___________________________

ON ___________________________

Lion of Judah

Star of David

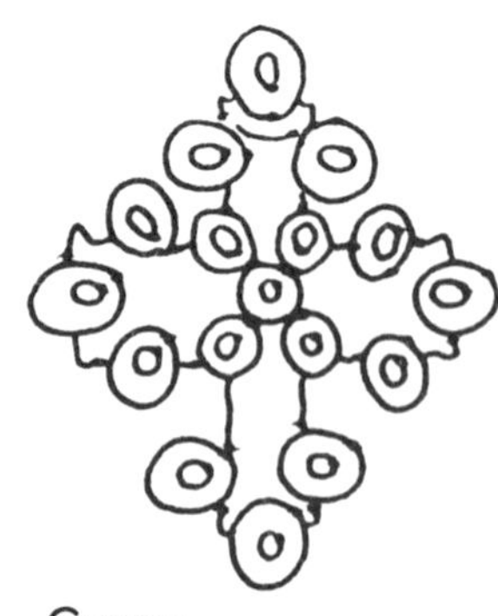

Cross

መጽ-ሐፍ ቅዱስ

Mets-Haf Kioous
(Holy Bible in Amharic script)

Hands in prayer

Name ____________________

Hinduism/Raksha Bandhan

Protection

Raksha Bandhan is a time when people think about caring for and protecting each other in a brotherly and sisterly way.

✤ Work in groups to think of ways that you can encourage mutual protection in your school. How can you make your school a more caring community?

We can ____

____

____

____

____

____

____

____

____

____

Name ____________________

The wise men and the elephant

It was six men of Hindustan,
To learning much inclined,
Who went to see the elephant
(Though all of them were blind),
That each by observation
Might satisfy his mind.

The first approached the elephant,
And, happening to fall
Against its broad and sturdy side,
At once began to bawl:
'Why bless me! but the elephant
Is very like a wall!'

The second, feeling at the tusk
Cried, 'Ho! what have we here
So very round and smooth and sharp?
To me it's mighty clear
This wonder of an elephant
Is very like a spear!'

The third approached the animal,
And, happening to take
The squirming trunk within his hands,
Thus boldly up he spake:
'I see', quoth he, 'the elephant
Is very like a snake!'

The fourth reached out his eager hand,
And felt about its knee
'What most this wondrous beast is like
Is mighty plain', quoth he;
'Tis clear enough the elephant
Is very like a tree!'

The fifth, who chanced to touch the ear,
Said, 'E'en the blindest man
Can tell what this resembles most;
Deny the fact who can,
This marvel of an elephant
Is very like a fan!'

The sixth no sooner had begun
About the beast to grope,
Than, seizing on the swinging tail
That fell within his scope
'I see', quoth he, 'the elephant
Is very like a rope!'

And so these wise men of Hindustan
Disputed loud and long,
Each in his own opinion
Exceeding stiff and strong;
Though each was partly in the right,
They all were in the wrong!

At least these men of Hindustan,
Who none of them had sight,
After quarelling about the elephant,
Over different parts they did fight.
When all these parts together came,
They all of them were right!

And so we see when arguing
The best of things to do
Is listen to the other men
And see their points of view!

By John Saxe

The wise men and the elephant

- Read the poem of the blind men and the elephant.
- Now draw the six objects that the men thought they were touching.

Name ______________________

Peacock mobile

The peacock is a traditional decoration.

- ✤ Draw a peacock on card and cut it out carefully.
- ✤ Use bright colours to decorate the peacock.
- ✤ Find the point of balance and attach a string to hang it up.
- ✤ Use several peacocks to make a mobile.

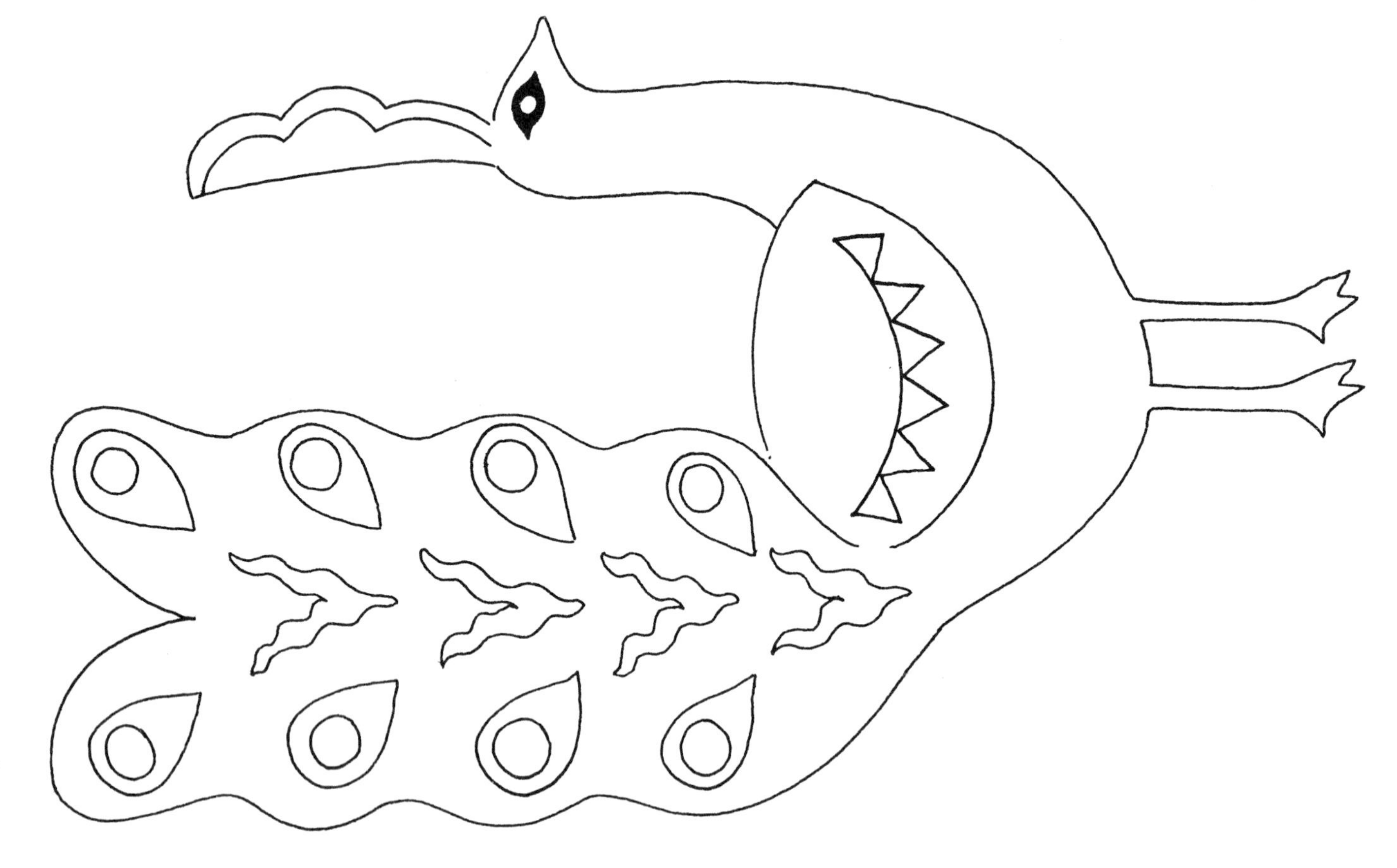